DRUG TESTS AND POLYGRAPHS

DRUG TESTS AND POLYGRAPHS

Essential Tools or Violations of Privacy?

DANIEL JUSSIM

Julian Messner Ⓜ New York
A Division of Simon & Schuster, Inc.

Published by Julian Messner
A Division of Simon & Schuster, Inc.
Simon & Schuster Building
Rockefeller Center
1230 Avenue of the Americas
New York, NY 10020

JULIAN MESSNER and colophon are
trademarks of Simon & Schuster, Inc.
Designed by Jean Wisenbaugh
Manufactured in the United States of America

Lib. ed. 10 9 8 7 6 5 4 3 2 1
Pbk. ed. 10 9 8 7 6 5 4 3 2 1

Library of Congress Cataloging in Publication Data

Jussim, Daniel.
  Drug tests and polygraphs.

  Bibliography: p.
  Includes index.
  Summary: Describes how drug and polygraph tests work, how they are being used, and
court cases involving them.
  1. Narcotic laws—United States—Juvenile literature.   2. Lie detectors and detection—
United States—Juvenile literature.   3. Privacy, Right of—United States—Juvenile litera-
ture.   [1. Narcotic laws.   2. Lie detectors and detection. 3. Privacy, Right of] I. Title.
KF3890.Z9J87 1987   363.2′52   87-11192

ISBN 0-671-64438-6 (Lib. ed.)
0-671-65977-4 (Pbk. ed.)

For my mother and sister

ACKNOWLEDGMENTS

The author acknowledges gratefully the help of Robert Ellis Smith, Loren Siegel, and Ari Korpivaara, who reviewed the manuscript and Sonia DiVittorio, who copyedited it. Thanks also to the following people for providing important material: Jon Bauer, Joseph Buckley, Judy Goldberg, Ed Martone, Norma Rollins, Elizabeth Schulman, Leonard Shrier, Howard Simon, Keith Snyder, Nadine Strossen, and Elizabeth Symonds.

CONTENTS

DRUG TESTS AND POLYGRAPHS

The Choice between Security and Privacy

Between lie detector tests and drug tests,
you wonder how anybody can get any work
done.
—Bryant Gumbel, *The Today Show*

The use of drug tests and lie detector tests in employment and other situations has skyrocketed over the last fifteen years in the United States. Employers want to rid workplaces of drug users and thieves, and many feel that these tests help them do that. Drug tests most often involve urinalysis, in which a urine specimen is sent to a lab for examination. In lie detector, or polygraph, tests, subjects are hooked up to a machine and quizzed by an examiner. As they answer the questions, the instrument draws a chart representing their physiological responses. Examiners use this chart to try to determine if the subject is lying or is being truthful.

The use of these tests has sparked controversy over their accuracy, their potential for discrimination, and their fairness in general. But the most important issues raised by widespread testing concern our privacy—do these examinations invade it, and how much of our privacy, if any, is worth giving up to get the benefits they may offer?

▶ In 1977, the Adolph Coors brewery used lie detector tests on job applicants in an apparent attempt to avoid hiring people it considered deviant. Examiners for Coors asked prospective employees the following questions: Have you ever participated in any type of march, riot, sit-in, or demonstration? What are your sexual preferences? How often do you change your underwear? Are you a Communist? The subsequent strike by Coors workers was partly in response to this effort.

▶ Without warning, in May 1986, authorities in Plainfield, New Jersey, rounded up all of the city's fire fighters, locked them into their station houses, and commanded them to give urine samples in front of their co-workers. The samples were sent to a laboratory and tested for drugs, and fire fighters showing evidence of drug use were given a choice: resign or face suspension and departmental charges. The fire fighters who failed the test sued their employer and won. Federal District Judge H. Lee Sarokin called mass drug testing "George Orwell's 'Big Brother' society come to life."

The federal judge was referring to Orwell's futuristic novel *1984*, which depicts a totalitarian society devoid of privacy. The omnipresent slogan "Big Brother is watching you" warned people to stay in line, to obey the rules at all times—for the eyes of the state were always open, observing their every move. The government's control was total and relentless; it even used "telescreens" in people's residences to keep an eye on them.

Could it happen here? Maybe not in any literal sense, but Orwell's tale was intended not so much to predict the future exactly, as to give a warning about what it might hold. And some people fear that we are becoming a society that has too much in common with Orwell's nightmare vision, that more and more of our privacy is being taken away, and that one day we will not have any at all. The Coors workers and the Plainfield fire fighters may very well have felt this way when confronted with their employer's testing tactics.

As technology has become more sophisticated, Americans have given up more privacy. Robert Ellis Smith, publisher of *Privacy Journal* and author of *Privacy: How to Protect What's Left of It,* points out that "it used to be easy to protect your privacy. You simply had to build a fence around your place and let the word get around that you 'valued your privacy.' . . . But in an age of computers and other sophisticated devices, it's no longer easy to protect your privacy."

One new development that has startling parallels with Orwell's novel is the use of a market survey technique in which people's television-viewing habits and purchasing patterns are monitored. The joint venture known as ScanAmerica pays households twenty dollars per month to be watched, in effect, by their televisions. About two-thirds of the families that are asked to participate go along with the request.

Family members agree to enter the number of the channel they are watching into a "people meter." And after they go shopping, the families also submit information on their purchases to ScanAmerica. Some market researchers hope that, eventually, members of participating families will wear sensors. These sensors could send signals when someone watches television identifying the person and giving data on his or her physiological and neurological responses to commercials.

While the ScanAmerica program is voluntary, it shows how willing many people are to relinquish their privacy. Or, looked at in another way, it illustrates "the natural cooperative nature of the American people"—in the words of one marketing expert.

But many times people must give up their privacy involuntarily. Security cameras are everywhere these days, even in some public restrooms. Applications for government benefits, such as student loans, or for a private benefit like a credit card require us to share information about our personal lives. This information is stored on computers from which it can be efficiently retrieved and possibly shared against our will. The growing use of drug tests and lie detectors in employment and other contexts also demands the surrender of some of our privacy.

There is usually a trade-off between privacy and something else we value. Security cameras may deter crime; computers increase efficiency; credit cards provide convenience; drug tests deter drug use; lie detectors may deter a variety of illicit activities. No one argues that the right to privacy is absolute—the question is, under what circumstances should we "cooperatively" give up this right, and when should we fight to keep it? Could it be more important to say no to drug tests and polygraphs than it is to say no to illegal drug use and other crimes? The fire fighters in Plainfield thought so, as did the Coors workers.

But there are competing values. Some argue that testing can work without being too intrusive, and that even if it must invade privacy somewhat, the ends justify the means. Our country has a stubborn drug problem. Some government officials and employers say that strategies used so far for solving it have largely failed, and that drug testing would go a long way toward ending illegal drug use. Businesses fed up with employee theft are placing their faith in the polygraph as one solution.

The debate pits the ideals of privacy and fairness against the practical demands of an unruly world in which testing is a tempting "quick fix." No policy will satisfy everyone, and as with other ethical and legal stand-offs, a line has to be drawn somewhere to balance competing interests.

As we study the various battles over testing, we should keep in mind that the controversy is uniquely American, made possible by our faith in technological devices as tools for solving social problems.

Our mystification by technology is well illustrated by the story of one employer's polygraph investigation into an employee theft in Cincinnati. In the middle of the test, the examiner left the subject alone with his results after telling him that responses so far indicated deception. The subject sat there nervously for a while. Then, all of a sudden, the man grabbed his polygraph charts, stuffed them in his mouth, chewed, and swallowed them. The examiner, who had actually observed the spectacle through a one-way mirror, returned, pretending that nothing had happened. He leaned down, put his ear to the polygraph, and exclaimed, "What's that? He ate them?" Horrified, the surprised subject said, "My God, you mean the thing can *talk,* too?" He then admitted that he was the thief.

Of course, not all Americans are this naive about technology. But we do tend to regard scientific inventions with more awe than people in other nations. No other country uses polygraph and drug tests to screen job applicants and employees. David Lykken, author of *A Tremor in the Blood: Uses and Abuses of the Lie Detector,* wrote, "Like Coca-Cola and the snowmobile, the lie detector has become a distinctive feature of contemporary American culture." Since he wrote that in 1981, urine tests for drugs have assumed a similar position.

PART 1
Drug Tests

CHAPTER 1

The Drug Problem: Can Tests Help?

*I*n spite of the many efforts to curb it, drug abuse continues to be a big problem in the United States, with great public health, social, and economic costs. Many call it an epidemic.

Close to a quarter of all Americans have smoked marijuana; 20 million get high on it regularly. Cocaine, or coke, is snorted, "free-based," or injected on a regular basis by between 5 million and 6 million of the country's population. An additional half million people are heroin addicts. Coke has taken marijuana's place as the middle class's "drug of choice," and the invention of an inexpensive, smokable form known as crack has made the drug widely available to the poor. While consumption levels of other illegal drugs are stable or decreasing, cocaine use is on the rise.

Cocaine is derived from the leaves of the South American coca plant and is the most powerful naturally occurring stimulant. Like other stimulants, it creates a feeling of euphoria and high self-esteem in the user. Chronic abuse produces anxiety and paranoia, restlessness, extreme irritability, and vivid hallucinations. Excessive doses may cause seizures, respiratory failure, and death.

Opium derivatives such as heroin and morphine act on the central nervous system and smooth muscles. Repeated use results in increasing tolerance to the drug, requiring progressively larger doses to get the same powerful high. It also causes a moderate to high degree of physical and psychological dependence. Side effects of these drugs include dizziness, nausea, and vomiting. Quitting "cold turkey" produces symptoms such as irritability, tremors, chills and sweating, severe muscle cramps, and nausea. Overdose can cause convulsions, coma, and death.

Besides health problems, drug abuse causes crime and social decay on several levels. Addicts steal to support their expensive habits. Drug traffickers smuggle, bribe, terrorize, and kill to transfer their product successfully. In March 1986, the President's Commission on Organized Crime labeled drug trafficking "the most serious organized crime problem in the world today."

In addition, drug abuse takes a toll in dollars and cents. The Research Triangle Institute, a respected North Carolina business-sponsored research organization, says that in 1983 illegal drug use cost the U.S. economy $60 billion; alcoholism cost $117 billion.

Government efforts to stop international traffickers from smuggling illegal drugs across our borders and to stop local pushers from selling them have accomplished little. "Law enforcement has been tested to its utmost," said Irving R. Kaufman, a judge on the U.S. Court of Appeals for the Second

Circuit who served as chairman of the Commission on Organized Crime. "But let's face it—it hasn't succeeded."

The failure to cripple the activities of pushers and traffickers and to convince people not to take drugs has led to a new strategy. Authorities reason that it is time to take the war on drugs to the users. If users can be easily identified, they will be deterred, the reasoning goes. If they're not deterred, they can be rehabilitated—or punished. As the demand for drugs decreases, the supply will dry up, and we will move closer to being a society free of illicit drugs. This is the vision of people favoring drug testing. It is what President Ronald Reagan had in mind when he signed an executive order in September 1986 calling for a "drug-free workplace" and requiring mandatory testing of as many as 1 million federal workers.

The drug-testing efforts that are so controversial today have their roots in a procedure practiced for many years at methadone clinics and other drug treatment centers to monitor the rehabilitation of addicts. In the 1970s, this procedure was put into use by the military. Responding to the high heroin-addiction rate among soldiers returning from Vietnam, the Department of Defense conducted drug screening to identify and treat them. In 1981, the military began massive drug screening of personnel. It is now the nation's biggest drug tester, with over 3 million tests given throughout its ranks each year.

Drug testing has spread in recent years thanks to the stubbornness of the drug problem and to the availability of cheap urine-testing kits. Today, tests for drugs are routinely administered to millions of workers in the public and private sectors in the hope of eliminating drugs in the workplace. Nearly 5 million Americans took drug tests in 1985. They worked in factories and offices, drove trucks and flew planes. According to the National Institute on Drug Abuse (NIDA), about one-third of the largest American companies test the urine of their employees or job applicants, seeking residues of ingested cocaine, marijuana, heroin, PCP, barbiturates, amphetamines, and other drugs.

The drug test of choice is currently urinalysis, but other tests exist that analyze blood, hair, saliva, brain waves, breath, or the subject's ability to walk a straight line. Most employers don't actually analyze urine samples on their premises, but send them off to a commercial laboratory. The labs first screen samples, commonly with an imprecise *immunoassay* test costing from two to five dollars per sample. Suspicious urine may then be subjected to a more rigorous procedure, such as *gas chromatography/mass spectrometry,* which costs about sixty to seventy dollars for each test. In the most commonly used immunoassay test—known as EMIT—special chemicals are added to the urine, causing a chemical reaction. The amount of light absorbed during the reaction clues technicians in to which drug is involved, if any. Another popular immunoassay test uses radioactive materials to spot drug residues, known as metabolites. Gas chromatography is more complicated; in its most precise form it breaks down the urine into individual ions.

Drug testing is a profitable business, with some U.S. pharmaceutical companies making high profits from the diagnostic tools they sell. The Syva Corporation, a subsidiary of the Syntex Corporation in Palo Alto, California, which sells the EMIT kit, and Hoffmann-La Roche in Nutley, New Jersey, have profited greatly. In 1985, they had the biggest shares of the multimillion dollar U.S. market for drug tests.

The first companies to implement drug testing were aerospace corporations, airlines, and railroads. Jumping on the bandwagon have been such prestigious firms as Exxon, IBM, Lockheed, Shearson Lehman Brothers, Federal Express, United Airlines, Hoffmann-La Roche, Du Pont, AT&T, and *The New York Times.* Major league baseball, the National Football League, and several other sports organizations, both professional and amateur, have testing programs as well.

Many government agencies on the federal, state, and local levels use drug screens, especially where public safety or national security is involved. Employees are not the only people being asked to submit to testing—students, prisoners, and arrestees have been targets as well. There is even a do-it-yourself home-testing kit that parents can use to see if their children take illegal drugs.

Different employers use drug tests in different ways. Some have voluntary testing programs, others require submission to testing as a condition of employment. Tests are most commonly used to screen job applicants. Some employers require employees to undergo periodic examinations, and some conduct random tests. Other employers will demand that a worker be tested only when they have reason to believe that the individual is using drugs.

The consequences of a positive test result—that is, one that may show evidence of illegal drug use—also vary from company to company. Applicants testing positive are generally not offered jobs, but are sometimes given a chance to reapply later. Employees who fail drug tests may be fired, disciplined, or required to enroll in a drug rehabilitation program. People who refuse to take a test when asked are usually fired or not hired. Some companies, like Southern Pacific Railroad, will foot the bill for most rehabilitation expenses.

THE CASE FOR DRUG TESTING

Employers are especially concerned about the effects of drugs. A March 1986 report in *Time* magazine said, ''Illegal drugs have become so pervasive in the U.S. workplace that they are used in almost every industry, the daily companions of blue- and white-collar workers alike. Their presence on the job is sapping the energy, honesty and reliability of the American labor force.'' Many employers say that drug use lowers worker productivity and increases absenteeism, as well as the risk of injury. In addition, employers complain that workers who use drugs make more medical claims, driving up the premiums of health insurance paid for by the company. And addicts are more likely to steal from their workplace to feed their expensive habits. Finally, employers say that when a worker's drug use results in him or her accidentally injuring someone else while on the job or on the road home, the company can be held responsible for damages in a lawsuit.

In the last ten years, drug or alcohol use among workers apparently led to fifty train accidents. These tragedies took the lives of thirty-seven people, injured eighty others, and cost $34 million in property damage. For example, in a 1979 incident that cost two lives and $467,500 in damages, a man driving a train for Conrail crashed into another train at Royersford, Pennsylvania. High on marijuana, he had taken the locomotive straight through a stop signal.

Defense industry executives worry that drugs could put our national security in jeopardy. They believe that users may construct faulty military equipment or sell classified information to get money to buy drugs.

According to federal experts, from 10 percent to 23 percent of American workers use dangerous drugs while on the job. And counselors at 800-COCAINE, a New Jersey–based hot line, found in a 1985 study that 75 percent of their callers took coke on the job, 69 percent regularly worked while high on the drug, and 25 percent used the white powder at work every day.

Many employers who use drug testing say that it has helped them get drugs out of their workplaces. Says Robert Angarola, a Washington, D.C., management attorney, "Quite often, people faced with a test will stop using drugs—85 to 90 percent of them—because they are so linked to their work." Commonwealth Edison, a Chicago-based electric utility, attributes some of the improvements in its workforce to an antidrug program that includes required urinalysis for job applicants. Since the program started, employees have missed fewer workdays, made fewer medical claims, and had fewer accidents while on the job, the company said. Other companies that have embraced drug testing point to improved work quality, discipline, and employee morale.

Private testing efforts are applauded by the federal government. Said Dr. Michael Walsh, chief of the clinical and behavioral pharmacology branch of NIDA, "We feel that if Big Business continues as it has in the last year to develop more and more stringent kinds of policies . . . it may be very effective in changing the way people view drug taking in this country." Walsh believes that drug testing will combat peer pressure to use drugs by giving people a good reason to say "no" to drugs.

Rear Admiral Paul Mulley, former head of the U.S. Navy's antidrug program, claimed that urine testing is "the number-one deterrent" to drug use. He said that the practice has led to a dramatic decrease in drug use in the Navy—from 48 percent of enlisted people in 1982 to 4 percent in 1986. "The great story in the Navy is that every other positive indicator went up—combat readiness, the retention rate, the reduction in accidents and injuries and illnesses. And . . . less than 1 percent of discharges resulted from [drug tests]." Thus, testing may be far more effective in decreasing demand for drugs than attempts to criminally prosecute users.

THE CASE AGAINST DRUG TESTING

Critics of drug testing argue that even if it does work as a deterrent, its costs far outweigh its benefits. They say that testing programs are unethical and sometimes illegal, and they are fighting them in the courts, in legislatures, and in union halls. These are some of their arguments:

▶ *Drug testing is a violation of privacy.* Because everyone has "the right to be let alone," and no authority has the right to arbitrarily search a person's bodily fluids. Further, by requiring that a urine specimen be produced in the presence of a witness, testing may humiliate subjects. And the procedure may reveal much information about an individual's health and bodily chemistry that he or she does not want to divulge. Finally, when carried out in employment situations, it monitors a worker's off-the-job activity, which is none of the boss's business. It is antithetical to the American sense of fair play to subject someone to such intrusions without having good grounds to suspect him or her of drug abuse.

▶ *Drug testing is unfair.* Because it is often inaccurate, indicating that a drug-free person has used an illegal substance. In addition, drug tests unfairly require people to prove that they do not use drugs—when they should be considered innocent until proven guilty.

▶ *Drug testing does not measure job impairment or performance.* Because urinalysis does not reveal whether a worker was high at the time he or she gave the sample. Urine may test "positive" for drugs ingested long before a sample is given.

▶ *Drug testing has negative political effects.* Because demagogues use the issue to get votes, avoiding intelligent debate over the drug problem.

▶ *Drug testing has negative social effects.* Because it ignores the alcohol problem and, further, fosters social control and bad worker-management relations.

The clash of views between proponents and opponents of drug testing has resulted in an intensely emotional battle dubbed "jar wars." It has pitted employers and their allies against civil libertarians and workers'-rights advocates. The next three chapters focus on the legal aspects of this fight:

Chapters 2 and 3 look at constitutional issues, which come into play most often in public sector employment, and Chapter 4 deals with legal issues raised by testing in private sector employment, schools, and the criminal justice system. Finally, Chapter 5 discusses some controversies over testing that will not be settled by lawyers and judges, but by the rest of us.

CHAPTER 2

Legal Issues: Privacy and the Fourth Amendment

*L*abor leaders and civil libertarians have attacked drug testing with mixed results in the courts. Most of the cases have involved the use of urinalysis by government employers. Because the U.S. Constitution controls the powers of federal, state, and local governments but not those of private employers, testing opponents have fared better in public sector cases. To a large extent, private companies are bound only by local and state law in their employment practices.

Civil libertarians (people concerned with the protection of constitutional rights) criticize drug testing done in certain circumstances as violating the constitutional protections provided in the Fourth Amendment. Meanwhile, employers insist that to a large extent these protections do not apply to drug testing in employment situations and maintain that it is their right to test workers.

The Fourth Amendment to the U.S. Constitution states, "The right of the people to be secure in their persons, houses, papers, and effects, against unreasonable searches and seizures, shall not be violated." It also says that a search warrant may only be issued when there is "probable cause" to believe that a search will turn up evidence that a suspect has done something illegal.

When the Founders wrote the Fourth Amendment into the Constitution's Bill of Rights, they were reacting to a hated British policy carried out against colonial America that allowed the King's custom inspectors to arbitrarily search colonists' homes and warehouses for smuggled goods. Smuggling was a common practice at a time when Britain demanded that the colonists pay extremely high import duties on any goods entering the colonies. Had the colonists been protected as we are by the Constitution, the British customs officials would have been required to obtain a court warrant for each search they conducted. To get one, they would have had to prove to a judge that they had objective evidence—"probable cause"— that led them to suspect a particular individual of possessing smuggled items. Thus, the Fourth Amendment attempts to spare innocent people the indignity of an intrusive search.

Not all searches are equal, however. For certain types of searches, there are exceptions to strict Fourth Amendment requirements. The courts will permit "administrative" searches without a warrant of individuals not held in suspicion. Administrative searches are carried out primarily to deter crime, not to prosecute someone for an illegal activity. Metal detectors in airports, which are used to search all passengers for weapons, qualify as administrative searches. They have been found to satisfy the "balancing test" courts use to determine if an administrative search is constitutional. This test weighs the need for the search against the search's invasiveness—how much it violates "the sanctities of a man's home and the privacies of life." The courts have found the government's need to prevent hijacking paramount and the invasiveness of metal detectors minimal.

Is taking a drug test like walking through a metal detector, legally speaking? One precedent-setting case with major implications for drug testing, *Schmerber* v. *California,* was decided by the U.S. Supreme Court in 1966. In this case, a California man named Armando Schmerber drove his car away from a bar where he had been drinking late at night. The car skidded, crossed the road, and smashed into a tree, injuring him. A police officer who arrived at the scene smelled liquor on Schmerber's breath and noticed that he was glassy eyed. Schmerber was taken to a hospital, treated for his injuries, and then arrested for driving while intoxicated. Against Schmerber's wishes, the arresting officer ordered a doctor at the hospital to take a blood sample and test it for alcohol; the sample showed Schmerber to be drunk.

At his trial, Schmerber said the results of the blood test should not be allowed as evidence against him. He argued that the test constituted a search without a warrant and thus violated his Fourth Amendment rights. Further, he said that being compelled to give a blood sample amounted to "self-incrimination." The Fifth Amendment to the Constitution protects people from self-incrimination—having to testify against themselves (see Chapter 3).

The Supreme Court threw out Schmerber's self-incrimination claim, finding that the Fifth Amendment applies only to written or spoken testimony. The Court also dismissed his Fourth Amendment claim. If the arresting officer had sought a search warrant, the Court held, the evidence—alcohol in the blood—would have disappeared. The need to do the test right away overrode any search-warrant requirement. But the Court's ruling stated that even though a warrant was not required in this case, blood testing for the presence of alcohol "plainly involves the broadly conceived reach of a search and seizure under the Fourth Amendment." If a test like this had been done in the absence of "a clear indication that in fact evidence will be found," it would have violated the Constitution. The "clear indication" in Schmerber's case was his obviously drunken state.

Schmerber v. *California* found searching a person's bodily fluids similar legally to searching a person's home. Mandatory drug tests in employment situations, however, could be considered administrative searches. Unlike the driver before the Supreme Court, employees who test positive for drugs do not face criminal punishment. They might lose a job, but they won't go to jail. If drug tests in employment situations were administrative searches, the courts would have to use the balancing test to decide which was the overriding concern—the threat to public and workplace safety posed by employees who use drugs or the rights of the innocent to be free from unreasonable searches.

In addition to protecting us against unreasonable searches and seizures, the Constitution gives citizens a more general guarantee of privacy. There is no actual use of the word *privacy* in the Constitution, but the Supreme Court has found this protection implicit in the Bill of Rights. It has used this guarantee in ruling in favor of citizens' rights to obtain contraceptives and abortion services.

Opponents of drug testing believe that an employer's need for a drug-free workplace never justifies screening done on any basis other than "individualized reasonable suspicion." "Not only is my home my castle," writes columnist William Safire in *The New York Times,* "my body is my citadel. Unless I give you probable cause to suspect me of a crime, what goes on in my home and body and mind is my business."

Yet some people favoring drug testing say that only the guilty should object to such a search—not the innocent, who have nothing to hide. Responding to this, Gary T. Marx, a sociology professor at the Massachusetts Institute of Technology, said, "We value envelopes around letters . . . not to protect illegality but because liberty is destroyed when such boundaries can be crossed at will."

Drug-testing proponents point to the enormity of the drug problem, which they feel overrides the privacy issue. "If we are going to curb the tidal wave of drugs pouring into this country, using illegal drugs must be unacceptable. Period. And that means on the job, at home, and at school," said Peter B. Bensinger, former federal drug enforcement administrator. Instead of looking at a worker's right to be let alone, Bensinger emphasizes the employer's responsibility to provide a safe workplace, an end, he feels, that can be reached with the aid of drug testing.

Lawyers defending drug testing compare it to blood tests for marriage license applicants, fingerprinting of workers, and background checks and physical examinations conducted to see if a prospective employee is fit for work. Generally, these procedures all pass constitutional muster. In an amicus brief filed to defend the drug testing of police officers in Boston, the U.S. Department of Justice said, "Employees have no recognized, absolute expectation of privacy that precludes an employer from conducting reasonable inquiries into an employee's fitness for duty." Attorney General Edwin Meese said that the Constitution doesn't apply to drug testing because "by definition . . . it's something the employee consents to as a condition of employment."

Besides being a search of bodily fluid, there are several other grounds on which drug tests may be considered invasive. These may add weight to the claim that such tests violate Fourth Amendment and other constitutional privacy rights.

For one thing, the tests sometimes involve observed urination. To be sure subjects don't cheat by tampering with a sample or substituting another person's urine, an employer may have someone watch them urinate. "If that is not done, it's a sham," says Dr. Robert Newman, president of Beth Israel Hospital in New York. Sometimes this procedure can be extremely abusive. Susan Register, who worked at a nuclear power plant in Georgia, described on the television program *Donahue* a urinalysis she took at work.

The first day I went they told me I could not give enough urine. The next day . . . the nurse took me into a bathroom, she told me we were going to do it differently today. She made me stand in the middle of the bathroom with my [right] hand in the air, with my pants around my ankles, with a bottle between my legs. She walked real close to me and leaned over. I was scared she was going to touch me. When she came back around I took my right hand down, got the bottle, because my [left] hand was soaking wet. I handed it to her. She screamed at me that I had not followed the procedure and was going to have to do it again. Well, needless to say, I did not do it again and I will never, if it means that I will never have a job again, I will never eat. I will never do that again. It could happen to you.

Of course, not all procedures are this extreme, but civil libertarians say that there is always a potential for such abuses and fear that incidents like this are common. In any case, they say, producing a urine sample while under observation is inherently embarrassing and humiliating. Drug-testing advocates say that abuses would be avoided if employers issued guidelines specifying how drug tests were to be carried out. "We want proper testing procedures to be performed," said Arthur Brill, who served as spokesman for the President's Commission on Organized Crime. In March 1986, the commission recommended a policy of mandatory drug testing for federal workers.

Another potentially invasive aspect of the tests is that they can reveal far more than whether or not a person has taken illicit drugs. They may give an employer detailed information on a subject's bodily chemistry that can reveal much about his or her life. Urinalysis can tell an employer if a worker is pregnant—or is being treated for heart disease, manic-depression, diabetes, epilepsy, or schizophrenia, among other conditions.

Urinalysis cannot show precisely *when* a drug was taken or how much of it was ingested. When drug metabolites are detected in the urine, it doesn't necessarily mean a drug is still in the bloodstream and having an effect. Marijuana metabolites, for example, may be present in urine more than one month after a joint is smoked. Civil libertarians say this causes two problems. First, it lets an employer monitor a worker's off-the-job activities. Said the American Civil Liberties Union (ACLU), a group that has brought many lawsuits against drug testing, "An employee who smokes a marijuana joint on a Saturday night may test positive the following Wednesday, long after the drug has ceased to have any effect. Why is what happened Saturday the employer's business?"

Employers say their workers have no business breaking the law. They also point to evidence suggesting that off-the-job drug-taking may affect on-the-job performance. One study, conducted by the Stanford University School of Medicine and the Palo Alto Veterans Administration Medical Center, indicated that marijuana could decrease someone's reaction time and mechanical ability for 24 hours after it is ingested. The study was done on pilots, using flight simulators. A day after getting high, the pilots could not manage a smooth landing. This study has been criticized for not using proper scientific controls. Its authors concede that the findings were merely "preliminary" and not conclusive.

A second problem with the fact that drug residues may show up in urine long after ingestion is that a urine test cannot actually measure the impairment or intoxication of a worker at the time it is administered. Thus, say drug-testing opponents, it does not help keep the workplace safer. Someone could test positive and still be in fine shape to work. On the other hand, because of the chemical characteristics of certain drugs, a very stoned individual could test negative. According to Dr. Ronald Seigel, a psychopharmacologist at the UCLA School of Medicine, someone could be almost "catatonic" from the hallucinogen PCP (angel dust) and still test negative. Conversely, he or she could test positive without being impaired.

Some experts question the extent to which drug use—especially casual use—impairs workers. Dr. Norman V. Kohn, chairman of the Department of Neurology at Mount Sinai

Hospital Medical Center, said, "Sleep deprivation and anxiety probably cause as much work impairment as drugs do." The ACLU argues that because urinalysis does not measure impairment, even people in high-risk jobs should not be compelled to undergo the procedure unless their employers have good grounds to suspect them of using drugs that are interfering with their performance: "It would be far more meaningful to require all airline pilots to undergo a brief neurological exam for impaired visual acuity or motor coordination before stepping into the cockpit. No one could object to that." Further, civil libertarians maintain that any good employer should be able to spot impaired workers just by observing them. "It's called the 'two-eyes test,' " said Loren Siegel, special assistant to the executive director of the ACLU.

Finally, civil libertarians worry about inaccurate test results ending up on a person's employment or insurance records and being shared through computers with other potential employers. "There is a potential for a high-tech type of blacklisting," said Jay Nickerson of the ACLU's Maryland chapter.

Most federal district courts and most state courts have ruled that testing public employees for drugs without reasonable grounds for suspecting them of using drugs violates their privacy. Urinalysis is not like a walk through an airport metal detector; it is more intrusive and less necessary, according to most judges. However, in the four cases reaching federal appeals courts—next to the Supreme Court, the highest level of courts in the nation—judges have found drug testing permissible under the Constitution.

One important ruling in *McDonell* v. *Hunter* involved the urinalysis of guards at an Iowa prison. The July 1985 decision was made by U.S. District Judge Harold Vietor. The plaintiff, Alan F. McDonell, a Department of Corrections employee, brought suit when he was fired for refusing to undergo urinalysis. Prison officials had asked him to take the test because, they said, he had been seen with an individual suspected by local law enforcement officials of selling drugs. When he started his job in 1979, he had signed a form permitting searches of prison employees for security reasons at any time.

In *Schmerber,* the Supreme Court had ruled on blood tests, not urine tests, so this was new territory for the judge. Judge Vietor ruled that urinalysis was in fact a search within the meaning of the Fourth Amendment because "one does not reasonably expect to discharge urine under circumstances making it available to others to collect and analyze in order to discover the personal physiological secrets it holds except as part of a medical examination." Because McDonell's simply being seen with someone under suspicion did not provide reasonable grounds to conduct a search, the judge ruled the urine test unconstitutional.

The defendants had argued that the test was reasonable because drug users are undesirable employees who are more likely than others to smuggle drugs to inmates. Victor agreed that testing might be valuable, but said that that would not make it legal: "Searches and seizures can yield a wealth of information useful to the searcher. (That is why King George III's men so frequently searched the colonists.) That potential, however, does not make a governmental employer's search of an employee a constitutionally reasonable one." The judge prohibited prison officials from carrying out urine testing in the absence of individualized reasonable suspicion. It did not matter, he said, that McDonell had signed a consent to be searched; the consent itself was an unreasonable condition of employment. Significantly, though, he did allow urinalysis for drugs as part of a pre-employment or periodic physical examination.

When the defendants in *McDonell* appealed the district court decision to the Eighth Circuit Court of Appeals, the presiding judges, by a two-to-one vote, narrowed considerably Vietor's ruling. They said that the attempted testing of McDonell was unconstitutional only because it was arbitrary. Random drug testing of guards is permissible, so long as it is systematic (as in a lottery), because "the institutional interest in prison security is a central one." This interest overrides the "limited intrusion into the guards' expectation of privacy."

There have been many other cases in which the courts have ruled against drug tests on Fourth Amendment grounds, with a number of decisions citing the district court ruling in *McDonell*. A New York State court rebuffed school officials in Long Island when they planned to test the urine of twenty-three teachers seeking tenure and then to expand the practice to cover administrators, newly hired teachers, and other employees. In a memo to the judge hearing the case, New York Civil Liberties Union Staff Attorney Richard Emery wrote, "Never before has any governmental authority asserted the expansive right to require teachers—one of society's most respected and trusted groups—to degrade themselves and their profession by compelled submission to a search of bodily fluids."

And in ruling against the unannounced mass drug-testing of fire fighters in Plainfield, New Jersey, discussed in the Introduction, Federal District Judge H. Lee Sarokin said, "It reports on a person's off-duty activities just as surely as someone had been present and watching. It is George Orwell's 'Big Brother' society come to life." Judge Sarokin acknowledged that there is a drug problem in America, but saw drug testing as a graver threat: "In order to win the war against drugs, we must not sacrifice the life of the Constitution in the battle."

A federal district judge in New Orleans ruled as "utterly repugnant to the Constitution" a U.S. Customs Service program that required employees seeking promotion to certain positions to undergo urinalysis. Judge Robert F. Collins said that, in addition to violating the Fourth Amendment, the program invaded the general "zone of privacy created by several fundamental constitutional guarantees."

Collins' ruling was reversed, however, by the Fifth Circuit Court of Appeals. This court agreed that urinalysis does indeed constitute a search under the Fourth Amendment, but found that "because of the strong governmental interest in employing individuals for key positions in drug enforcement who themselves are not drug users and the limited intrusiveness of this particular program, it is reasonable and, therefore, is not unconstitutional."

Another victory for drug testing came in a case involving horse racing, *Shoemaker* v. *Handel*. Five famous jockeys, including William Shoemaker and Angel Cordero, sued over the New Jersey Racing Commission's urinalysis policy. They said the commission could test them only upon reasonable suspicion— it had no right to pick jockeys' names at random from an envelope to determine who would be tested when the final race of the day was over. The Court of Appeals for the Third Circuit upheld the racing commission's policy in July 1986 on the grounds that Fourth Amendment protections are weaker in a highly regulated industry with a history of corruption. The court said that the state had a "strong interest in assuring the public of the integrity of the persons engaged in the horse-racing industry."

The precedent for such random searches was set in 1972 in a case involving the inspection of gun dealers. The Supreme Court ruled then that inspectors needed neither reasonable suspicion nor a warrant because, as Judge Irving R. Kaufman explains, "pervasive Government regulation and licensing reduced the dealers' legitimate expectation of privacy. Unannounced periodic inspections were essential if the law was to serve as a credible deterrent." The plaintiffs in *Shoemaker* tried to appeal, but the Supreme Court refused to take the case.

Military courts permit random testing in the armed forces, where it is used extensively. While these courts recognize constitutional prohibitions against unreasonable searches and seizures, they sometimes use different standards for deciding what is "reasonable" than civilian courts.

The military courts, however, do insist that fair procedures be carried out. In 1984, the Army told about ninety thousand soldiers who had tested positive that these results were questionable. A panel of Army and civilian experts said that drug tests given in 1982 and 1983 were not scientifically or legally supportable for use in disciplinary actions. The results had become part of soldiers' permanent records, with some having led to less-than-honorable discharges. After the panel's decision, the Army allowed soldiers to appeal blemishes on their record resulting from the questionable tests. According to the ACLU, invalid testing remains a problem in the military.

The right to have testing administered fairly is called a due-process protection. Due process comes into play even when the Fourth Amendment does not. This legal concept is discussed in the next chapter.

CHAPTER 3

Legal Issues: Due Process, Self-incrimination, Discrimination

For public-sector drug tests to be upheld in court, they must pass several legal criteria besides the Fourth Amendment and other constitutional privacy protections. Chief among these is *due process*—the right to have legal proceedings against you carried out in accordance with established rules and principles—as guaranteed by the Constitution.

DUE PROCESS

The Fifth and Fourteenth Amendments to the Constitution provide that no government may "deprive any person of life, liberty, or property without due process of law." This guarantees the basic fairness of legal proceedings. Critics of drug testing say that because urinalysis is often inaccurate, it violates due process when used in the public sector. Defenders of the procedure maintain that it is possible to reach accuracy rates of 100 percent.

Everyone agrees that the initial screening tests used to check for drug metabolites are somewhat inaccurate. Even the Syva Corporation, a pharmaceutical firm that claims a 97 percent to 99 percent accuracy rate for the drug screen it manufactures, warns that a back-up test must be done on all samples yielding positive results. But not all employers are willing to pay for the more expensive confirmation. This can result in ''false positives''—the labeling of drug-free people as users—and cost innocent workers their livelihoods.

Performing confirmation tests would mean fewer false positives, but critics say that mistakes at the laboratory caused by human error are always possible—samples get mixed up, jars mislabeled, and equipment inadequately cleaned. They point to a 1985 report by the federal Centers for Disease Control that appeared in the *Journal of the American Medical Association.* The report, which described a study of laboratories serving methadone treatment centers, concluded that there was a ''crisis in drug testing.'' In the study, scientists secretly added illegal drugs to hundreds of urine samples and sent them off to labs for testing. Only one out of eleven labs met acceptable performance standards for barbiturates, zero out of twelve for amphetamines, six out of twelve for methadone, one out of eleven for cocaine, two out of thirteen for codeine, and one out of thirteen for morphine. False positive error rates at the labs ran as high as 66 percent. Other studies have come up with similar results. Thanks to lab error rates reaching 97 percent in early military drug testing, the Navy reinstated four thousand sailors discharged for allegedly using drugs. Many others were not accepted back, but insisted they did not use drugs.

''The tests are very easy to do badly and very difficult to do well,'' said Dr. Bryan S. Finkle, a leading toxicologist at the

University of Utah in Salt Lake City. And Dr. Don H. Catlin, chief of clinical pharmacology at the University of California at Los Angeles, said that drug-testing firms "vary tremendously in quality from laboratory to laboratory as well as within the same laboratory on a day-to-day basis because the tests require skill in interpretation, and the reliability of the results depends on who does the test." Critics of testing worry that as the practice increases, laboratories will face increased competition and will cut quality controls even more.

Besides poor lab techniques, various foods and legitimate drugs may throw off drug-test results. Loren Siegel of the American Civil Liberties Union tells a story about some soldiers at Fort Dix who tested positive for marijuana after drinking ginseng tea. It turned out that there were minute quantities of THC—marijuana's active chemical ingredient—in the tea. Other people have tested positive for heroin after eating poppyseed cookies. And Dr. Douglas Lewis, head of the laboratory at Children's Memorial Hospital in Chicago, found that of one hundred football players his lab tested for drugs using Syva Corporation's EMIT test, thirty-five tested positive for marijuana because they had taken the anti-inflammatory drug ibuprofen. Ibuprofen is found in Advil and other over-the-counter pain relief medications.

There is also the problem of unintentional consumption of drugs, particularly smokable ones. "Small amounts of unlawful substances does not indicate the employee has a problem at all," said Alfred Klein, a Los Angeles management attorney. "In Southern California, where I live, it is not uncommon for marijuana smoke to blow into your face in public places, such as at outdoor concerts," he said. "And I'm not talking about rock concerts. I'm talking about the Los Angeles Philharmonic at the Hollywood Bowl."

Drug testing proponents say that any technical problems can be overcome. Noting the "passive inhalation" problem, for instance, Hoffmann-La Roche and the Syva Corporation warn labs not to label "positive" drug tests showing tiny amounts of marijuana metabolite. Before administering the test, some employers ask workers about substances they've used that might confound test results. And Dr. Michael Walsh of the National Institute on Drug Abuse insists that with proper quality control, urinalysis can be almost foolproof. Some experts have proposed laboratory certification as a way to insure the accuracy of the tests.

Courts have taken accuracy problems into account in rulings on drug testing. In the U.S. Customs Service case discussed in Chapter 2, Judge Robert F. Collins found that the drug-testing plan was "far from an infallible system." He cited the expert-witness testimony of a toxicologist who said that no matter how sophisticated, "all drug testing procedures result in false positives." He also noted the affidavit of customs worker Benito D. Juarez, who had already been tested:

> After I urinated, I noticed that the laboratory representative was affixing a sticker to my sample bottle. The sticker . . . had the wrong social security number on it. He had already filled out the labels before collecting our samples, and apparently he placed Fred Robinson's sticker on my bottle. When I alerted him to his mistake, he went back and checked his papers to determine my social security number and then corrected his error.

Other aspects of drug testing that involve due process do not bear on the accuracy of the procedure. For example, if employers tested workers without telling them, that would violate their due-process rights. According to Kurt Dubowski, a professor of forensic toxicology at the University of Oklahoma, this happens frequently. The employers use a urine sample provided at a routine pre-employment physical exam. Dubowski calls this practice "particularly unacceptable," because a rejected job applicant cannot contest the result.

Due process of law also contains the principle that people are to be considered innocent until proven guilty. Civil libertarians charge that drug testing turns this concept on its head, making people guilty until they prove themselves innocent. As *New York Times* columnist William Safire says, "Rather than go to all the trouble of finding the guilty needle in the haystack, they prefer to force each piece of hay to prove it did nothing wrong. . . . To protect myself against terrorists, I will walk through a metal detector with fellow passengers—but that special circumstance must not be twisted into a precedent that shifts the burden of proof from the Government to the individual."

Some unions point out that not being presumed innocent can hurt people in a very direct way. John Dineen, president of Chicago Lodge 7 of the Fraternal Order of Police, says that district commanders require any police officer whom they don't like to take a drug test. "That puts a cloak of suspicion over him. Eighty-five to 90 percent of these officers come back clean, but the other officers say, 'If he had to go to a screen, there must be something to it.' That's not right."

People favoring drug testing typically argue that people who have done nothing wrong have nothing to fear. They claim that the civil libertarian position merely protects the guilty and punishes the innocent—those non-drug-users who suffer from the social and economic problems caused by drug abuse. *The New York Times,* which subjects its job applicants to a drug screen, pointed out in an editorial that "the presumption of innocence applies automatically only in the case of criminal prosecutions." As we saw in Chapter 2 regarding the operation of the Fourth Amendment, since drug testing in an employment context has less severe consequences for the accused than testing in a criminal context, the constitutional restraints on it may be more relaxed.

SELF-INCRIMINATION

The Fifth Amendment to the Constitution says that no one "shall be compelled in any criminal case to be a witness against himself." People called as witnesses in a criminal case can "plead the Fifth"—refuse to respond to questions on the grounds that their answers may incriminate them. Some people feel that workplace drug testing forces people, on pain of losing their livelihoods, to incriminate themselves. *New York Times* columnist Russell Baker wrote satirically, "When Hitler and Stalin flourished, Americans were horrified by stories about good Nazi and good Communist children betraying their parents to the police. That was a long time ago, and we have changed since then." Now, Baker says, authorities are quick to let an individual's urine do the betraying, "making the body destroy the man."

In the Plainfield, New Jersey, case, officials told fire fighters that any positive drug-test results would possibly be turned over to the police. Thus, although the targeted fire fighters would be providing urine samples in an employment situation, the samples could theoretically incriminate them in court. Ira Glasser, executive director of the ACLU, maintains that even if an employer wished to guarantee the confidentiality of test results, it might not be possible to do so if a government prosecutor subpoenaed them in the course of a criminal investigation. However, as Judge Irving R. Kaufman points out, "Unlike possession and distribution of illegal drugs, use alone is generally not an indictable offense." It may be that the discovery of drug metabolites in someone's urine would not land him or her directly in jail. But it is conceivable that a positive test could advance a prosecutor's case against a suspect. For example, it might provide the "probable cause" needed to search the person's house.

Drug-testing advocates again argue that the Fifth Amendment doesn't apply in this situation. President Ronald Reagan stated during a 1986 press conference that since drug testing in the government was intended to identify and rehabilitate users, his plan to test federal employees was "not a case of saying that we're now going to find a way to . . . have people incriminate themselves so they can be fired or anything else."

Under *Schmerber* v. *California,* turning over bodily fluids to authorities does not legally constitute self-incrimination—the Fifth Amendment applies only to written or spoken testimony. But in the Customs Service case, Judge Collins ruled that the drug-testing plan violated the Constitution because it required workers to fill out a pretest form stating which legal and illegal drugs they had taken within the last thirty days. The information on this form could be used against them and was thus covered by the self-incrimination clause of the Fifth Amendment, Collins said.

DISCRIMINATION

Civil libertarians say that drug tests may be used to discriminate against "whistle-blowers"—workers who expose wrongdoing on the part of their employer. This may deprive the workers of their freedom of speech, which is guaranteed by the First Amendment to the Constitution. Several workers at a nuclear power plant in Georgia claimed that their employer subjected them to testing in order to silence them. One of these employees was Susan Register, whose account of her ordeal giving a urine sample was quoted in Chapter 2. The workers said that their employer provided a hot line on which employees could call in anonymous allegations of drug abuse by their colleagues. Accused workers were then forced to take a urinalysis. The employees bringing suit said they were fired for refusing to take or for failing the test. They maintain that they were turned in on the hot line because they had complained to the Nuclear Regulatory Commission about dangerous conditions at the plant.

Some disabled workers face two possible sources of discrimination. First, an employer may learn of the disability when the urine test reveals a prescription drug taken to treat it. Dr. Harold Bates, director of client relations and a toxicologist for Metpath Laboratories in Teterboro, New Jersey, said, "A company may be tempted to get rid of workers with medical problems, even though they may be doing a perfectly good job." He said that one company fired a worker after learning through urinalysis that he had asthma.

Second, it is possible that a urinalysis could "read" incorrectly a prescription drug taken for a disability and indicate that the test subject had ingested an illegal drug. The most commonly used urine tests cannot distinguish between certain legitimate prescription medications and illegal drugs. An employer who used these tests might deny a disabled person employment as a result. A lawsuit brought against the U.S. Post Office in Philadelphia said that its urinalysis procedure was illegal because of this flaw: it could mistake the metabolites of prescription drugs taken for conditions such as epilepsy for illegal-substance residues. The suit alleged that the post office was thus violating the Federal Rehabilitation Act of 1973 prohibiting discrimination against the disabled.

CHAPTER 4

Legal Issues: Private Sector, Schools, Criminal Justice System

Unlike testing in the public sector, urinalysis for drugs conducted in private employment raises narrow legal issues that do not involve the federal Constitution. In this chapter, we will examine these issues as well as questions arising out of testing conducted not in employment situations, but in schools, in prisons, and on the nation's roads and highways.

PRIVATE SECTOR

Employees of private companies do not have the same powerful constitutional protections against their employers as do government workers. Private-sector workers are, to a large extent, employed "at will," which means that companies need not provide a justification for dismissing them. Generally, the degree to which their on-the-job privacy and due-process rights are respected is at the discretion of management. Thus, if a company wants to fire all workers who fail a drug test, without letting them appeal the results, it often can. Nevertheless, civil libertarians argue that private employers should refrain from drug testing as a matter of principle—that even though they are not *legally* bound by the U.S. Constitution, they should be *morally* required to obey its ideals. Many private employers maintain that testing is their right; but some employees have found legal recourse in situations where they felt they were treated unfairly as a result of a drug test.

For instance, some have claimed that a drug test unfairly harmed their reputation, or slandered them. Since a positive result may damage someone's reputation, if the results can be proven inaccurate, there may be good grounds for a lawsuit.

In 1977, a railroad switchman sued a Houston railway company for defamation. He had passed out on the job, and the company had sent him to a doctor, who administered a urinalysis. Management said the test was positive for methadone, a drug used in the treatment of heroin addiction. The switchman's personal doctor ran his own test and reported that there was no methadone in the urine. Nevertheless, the company fired him for being a hazard. The switchman's lawsuit alleged slander, and a jury agreed, awarding him $200,000 in damages.

Private-sector workers living in states with special privacy protections in their *state* constitutions may find additional grounds for lawsuits. Californians voted in 1972 to amend their state constitution specifically to protect privacy. The amendment applies to the practices of private as well as public employers. The California courts have interpreted the amendment as being spurred by "the accelerating encroachment in personal freedom and security caused by increased surveillance and data collection activity in contemporary society." This activity leads to "overbroad collection and retention of unnecessary personal information by government and business interests." Only those privacy violations "justified by a compelling interest" are permitted under the amendment.

In September 1986, Collette Clark sued her employer, the San Diego Gas & Electric Company (SDG&E), for violating her privacy, which she asserted was protected under California's state constitution. SDG&E drug-tested Clark, a single parent, when she applied for a promotion from her clerical job with the utility company. The urinalysis supposedly revealed that she had smoked marijuana, and the company fired her. Clark insisted that she was drug free. Represented by the ACLU, she filed suit to get her job back and to halt the testing program. Meanwhile, she was forced to take a job as a waitress to support her child.

In a settlement with the plaintiff, SDG&E admitted that there "were problems with the test" they had used. The company issued a letter of apology to Clark and paid her an undisclosed sum as compensation for "pain and anguish." The apology said the urine sample may have been contaminated and that the laboratory to which it had been sent failed to perform a second test to confirm the results.

Elizabeth Schulman, the lawyer representing Clark, said of this case: "The problems with these tests have been shown over and over. As with my client, employees can be put in untenable positions by unreliable testing that result in tragic changes in their lives. . . . Collette went from a $6.00-an-hour job to waiting on tables for $3.50 an hour." Schulman also praised SDG&E for acting quickly after suit was filed to rectify the situation.

The company did not, however, agree to halt its testing program, though it did switch labs. Officials also said that they would take into consideration Clark's "feelings about maximizing privacy and human dignity whenever drug testing is performed."

A San Francisco lawsuit, *Luck* v. *Southern Pacific Transportation Company*, led to that city's passing legislation to ban drug tests. Barbara A. Luck, a computer programmer with the company for over six years, refused to take a urinalysis. Southern Pacific demanded that all its employees submit to the test and fired her for refusing, although they did not suspect her and considered Luck an excellent employee. Luck sued for wrongful termination and for invasion of privacy.

Southern Pacific argued that even though public safety was not at stake, their program served a legitimate business interest and was thus justified. Luck maintained that her former employer's need to ferret out drug users was not compelling enough to invade her privacy. As of this writing, the case has not yet been decided.

Amid the controversy stirred by Barbara Luck's suit, San Francisco became the first jurisdiction in the United States to pass legislation banning drug tests. The San Francisco Board of Supervisors in December 1985 amended their municipal code, saying, "It is the public policy of San Francisco that all citizens enjoy the full benefit of the right to privacy in the workplace guaranteed to them by the California Constitution. It is the purpose of this Article to protect employees against unreasonable inquiry and investigation into off-the-job conduct, association, and activities not directly related to the actual performance of job responsibilities." The legislation bars on-the-job drug tests except when the test meets three conditions: (1) the employer must have reasonable grounds for suspecting a worker to be impaired, (2) the worker's impairment has to constitute a "clear and present danger" to workplace safety, and (3) the employer has to give the worker a chance to contest the test results and to have bodily fluid specimens retested by a state-licensed laboratory.

The legislation does not prohibit the drug testing of job applicants. Nationwide, job applicants are the group most often tested, yet they generally have the least legal protection. Even unions cannot help them, since they do not become members until hired.

The ACLU is suing on behalf of an applicant for a sales job on Long Island who was not hired because he tested positive for opiates (morphine, heroin). He had been offered the job pending the results of a urinalysis. He says his dentist gave him codeine for root-canal work earlier in the day that he gave his urine sample, and this confused the test results. When he brought a prescription from his dentist, it did not change the company's mind.

To avoid situations like this, the state of Maine considered antitesting legislation that would cover job applicants. In January 1987, a special commission recommended that Maine's State Legislature forbid drug testing except breath-alcohol testing for applicants or workers—even those suspected of drug use. The only exception would be nuclear power plant employees. The commission urged the banning on the grounds that the tests are unreliable. "Inaccuracy rates are alarming," said Edith S. Beaulieu, the commission leader. The commission was also concerned about privacy and employer power, criticizing the tests as giving bosses "the job of medical experts, cops, judge, and jury." Finally, the commission noted that alcohol use among employees was more common than illegal drug use, but was eliciting less concern.

Jim A. McGregor, a dissenter on the commission, said testing was necessary: "Industry can find no other tool to fight the problem. Business and industry have a right to expect workers to come through their gates clean."

The Maine legislature followed the commission's recommendation to ban most drug testing, but the state's governor disapproved, and vetoed the bill. However, at least three other states—Iowa, Vermont, and Montana—now have laws curtailing drug testing in both public and private employment.

Most unions oppose drug testing done without individualized suspicion, and many have been able to protect their members against it. An important case involved urinalysis carried out on players in the National Football League, who are all members of the NFL Players Association, a union.

The union and management had an agreement dating back to 1982 governing the detection of player drug abuse and the education and treatment of those on drugs. Under the agreement, managers of NFL clubs could have a physician administer urinalysis for drugs during the preseason medical examination and also when they had reasonable cause to suspect a player of using drugs. After the 1986 Super Bowl, in which the Chicago Bears humiliated the New England Patriots, NFL Commissioner Pete Rozelle tried to alter this agreement. He made his plan in the wake of allegations that several players on the Patriots team had drug problems. The most controversial aspect of the plan called for all players to submit to two unscheduled drug tests during the football season.

The matter was put to arbitration. The NFL said such testing was necessary: without it, "players would be free to decide for themselves whether to consume illegal drugs, notwithstanding that drug use violates League rules and the players' contract commitments, directly imperils players' health and careers, lessens their athletic ability, harms their team's ability to compete, damages the League's image, and injures the public perception of the integrity of the League's product." The NFL also argued that players are role models for youth, who are particularly vulnerable to drugs.

The Players Association maintained that the NFL had no legal right to alter its 1982 agreement with the union. David Meggyesy, union director for the Western division, said players saw testing as "a control issue" and felt it violated their rights.

In his ruling, arbitrator Richard R. Kasher found that the Players Association, "contrary to popular media and public misconception," was making suitable efforts to stem drug abuse among players. He agreed with the union that management was bound by the 1982 agreement as far as drug testing was concerned.

SCHOOLS

A couple of public schools have attempted to institute drug-testing programs, but courts have frowned on the idea. Like public employees, public school students are protected by the U.S. Constitution. In December 1985, a New Jersey superior court ruled unconstitutional a testing plan proposed by school officials at Henry P. Becton Regional High School in East Rutherford, New Jersey. The plan would have subjected students to urine and blood testing for drugs and alcohol as part of an annual physical exam. Students who tested positive for drugs would have been suspended or expelled. The ACLU of New Jersey brought suit on behalf of five students opposing the tests.

Judge Peter Ciolino ruled that the school's proposed policy would violate the right of students to be free from unreasonable search and seizure as well as their due-process rights and "legitimate expectation of privacy and personal security." Ciolino rejected the school board's claim that drug use is a disease like any other and that authorities should have a free hand to test for it. "[This] policy," he wrote, "is an attempt to control student discipline under the guise of a medical procedure, thereby circumventing strict due-process requirements." If any problem could be classified as medical, then "medical testing is without limits," the judge argued. He also countered the board's contention that no individual suspicion is needed under its policy because all students would be tested, pointing out that the Fourth Amendment "is not limited to only those who are suspected of criminal behavior."

Students opposed the plan from the start. In a poll, 80 percent of them said it shouldn't be implemented. Carla Odenheim, the lead plaintiff in the case, said, "There really isn't [a drug problem] in my school. I think what they're saying is that anyone under eighteen doesn't have a right to anything, least of all their own body. They already have cameras on the buses. [Video cameras were installed in the district's school buses to keep an eye on unruly students.] What's next? Are they going to put cameras in the bathrooms to see if we're smoking? How about strip searches?''

Judith Campbell, mother of a Becton student, joined the suit because she felt that the testing policy trampled on her parental prerogatives and on her child's right to be presumed innocent. She said that ''education is the key'' to preventing drug abuse. ''The ones who are taking the drugs will find a way around drug testing.''

Other parents saw the plan as an important weapon against drug abuse. ''The hell with their constitutional rights,'' one said. ''Drugs are illegal. Once you do something illegal, you lose some of your constitutional rights.''

Becton's lawyer, who had hoped that the judge, as a parent, ''would have the courage of his convictions,'' felt instead that ''he took a very cautious, liberal view of the Constitution.''

In Arkadelphia, Arkansas, another judge struck down student drug testing. Judge Franklin Waters ruled, ''Requiring teenage students to disrobe from the waist down while an adult official watches the student urinate in the 'open' into a tube is an excessive intrusion under the Fourth Amendment.''

CRIMINAL JUSTICE SYSTEM

A police officer cannot come up to a person walking down the street who is behaving suspiciously and ask him or her to submit to a drug test. The results of such a test would be useless, because being intoxicated is not a crime. But there are two places where drug testing by law-enforcement officials *is* carried out: on the road, usually to check for drunk drivers, and in the prison system, to monitor the behavior of arrestees and inmates.

ROADBLOCKS

In the past, police fought drunk driving only by pursuing people whose driving looked suspicious, making them pull their cars off the road, and giving them breath-alcohol tests or walk-a-straight-line tests. Drivers showing evidence of intoxication were sent to the police station to be tested further and charged with a driving-while-intoxicated offense.

In the 1980s, though, many states, in an effort to crack down on drunk driving, added to their arsenals temporary "sobriety checkpoints"—drunk-driving roadblocks. Typically, roadblocks go up at night and are located in trouble spots where there are frequent alcohol-related accidents or arrests. They are highly visible, with warning signs, flashing lights, flares, police cars, and uniformed officers. Instead of stopping people who are driving suspiciously, these officers generally make all drivers pull over or use a formula, such as every fifth car. This avoids the illegal discrimination against individual drivers that would occur if police singled people out on some arbitrary basis—such as the color of their skin or the length of their hair. The police question the drivers and test those who appear to be intoxicated.

Proponents of roadblocks say they're a powerful weapon against drunk driving. For instance, the New York Governor's Alcohol and Highway Safety Task Force, made up of police officials, prosecutors, and members of citizens groups like Mothers Against Drunk Driving (MADD), argued that a roadblock "is the single most effective action in raising the community's perception of the risk of being detected and apprehended for drunk driving." But to those against roadblocks, they are too high a price to pay in liberty. They contend that police like using checkpoints because the stops enable them to arrest people—people whom they would not have otherwise been able to detain—for offenses not involving drunk driving. Said television commentator Andy Rooney, "I find this Gestapo-like invasion of privacy intolerable." Critics also say that traditional methods are more effective in catching intoxicated drivers.

No federal courts have ruled on the constitutionality of these new roadblocks, and state court decisions have been split. In a California case decided in September 1986, a state court found roadblocks unconstitutional. Richard T., the plaintiff, brought the case after being arrested at a roadblock in the early morning of a New Years Day in the city of Anaheim. An officer at the roadblock had smelled liquor on his breath and asked where he had been. When he answered, "a party," he was given an alcohol test and arrested. He moved to have the evidence against him discounted on the grounds that it was obtained in violation of the Fourth Amendment.

The court agreed, saying that the stopping and detention of a vehicle is a "seizure" under the Fourth Amendment. The court referred to the 1979 decision in *Delaware* v. *Prouse,* in which the U.S. Supreme Court ruled that "roving patrols," in which police stopped cars arbitrarily to check driver's licenses and car registration, violated the Fourth Amendment. While the Anaheim roadblock avoided being arbitrary by stopping each vehicle or every other vehicle, it was still unconstitutional. Unlike *fixed* checkpoints, such as airport metal detectors or border crossings between countries, temporary checkpoints "take the motorist by surprise" in an attempt to catch him or her breaking the law. Thus, they don't qualify for the administrative search exception to the Fourth Amendment; stopping a car at a roadblock is only legal when police have grounds to believe that the driver is intoxicated.

The court quoted legal scholars James B. Jacobs and Nadine Strossen, who wrote of roadblocks: "Neither Border Patrol checkpoint stops nor any other types of suspicionless investigations that the Supreme Court has authorized have touched the lives of so many citizens or been aimed at criminal enforcement. . . . Routine roadblocks call to mind the way police and soldiers are deployed in authoritarian societies."

Other state courts, such as those in Massachusetts, have held that temporary roadblocks do not raise constitutional concerns, as long as drivers are stopped by formula and other fair procedures are followed. A new procedure, called a "drugnet," is yet to be ruled on by any court. The ACLU has filed suit to halt temporary roadblocks—for drugs—used on the George Washington Bridge, which crosses the Hudson River between New York and New Jersey. At this checkpoint, police ask those suspected of being intoxicated but who are not under the influence of alcohol to provide a urine sample to be tested for drugs. Anyone who refuses is asked for a blood sample. If he or she refuses this, police take the suspect to a nearby hospital, where the blood sample is taken involuntarily.

PRISONS

Prison officials often administer random urine tests to inmates to deter drug use. Positive results may be used against prisoners in disciplinary proceedings, causing such adverse consequences as isolation, removal to a higher-security prison, or a decreased chance of getting parole. And sometimes drug tests are a condition of parole or probation, so that people who have been sentenced but permitted to stay out of jail are required to report for periodic drug testing.

Prisoners have fewer constitutional protections than other citizens, so it is hard for them to raise Fourth Amendment issues when protesting the tests. Under a 1976 Supreme Court decision in *Wolff* v. *McDonnell,* however, prisoners do not lose all of their constitutional rights upon incarceration. They are still entitled to fair treatment and some level of due process.

Thus, prisoners in several states have successfully fought testing programs in which the urinalysis administered was inadequate to prove wrongdoing. In Massachusetts, Superior Court Judge Hiller B. Zobel ruled that prisoners could not be punished on the basis of a positive EMIT urine test, because the test, used alone, is not reliable. "Admissibility of evidence deduced from a scientific discovery or device depends upon a showing by the proponent that scientists . . . have accepted it as reliable,'' he ruled. Since testimony failed to do this, the evidence was inadmissible. Its inadmissibility was not outweighed by prison officials' claim that "since the use of the Syva system within the institution, inmates rarely contest the test results and the number of inmates who plead guilty to drug charges at disciplinary hearings have increased dramatically.'' Zobel did not bar drug tests, but said EMITs had to be confirmed by a reliable method.

Several jurisdictions have instituted programs for pretrial drug testing of people charged with crimes. New York City and Indianapolis test adult arrestees, and Washington, D.C., which had likewise been testing adults since 1983, began testing juvenile arrestees as well in 1986.

In the District of Columbia, all arrestees are tested once before their bail hearing and may be tested again while awaiting trial. Positive results are not used to prosecute them, but may be used against them by judges when setting bail and terms of release. Jay Carver of the Pretrial Services Agency said that drug users are much more likely to fail to show up in court for their trial than nonusers.

Proponents of the District of Columbia's program also point to research showing that criminals commit four to six times more crimes when using drugs, and that drugs often give people the courage to break the law. Referring those who test positive to rehabilitation programs should thus cut down on crime. "The bottom line is public safety,'' said James K. Stewart, director of the National Institute of Justice. Officials claim that thanks to the drug-testing program, fewer people are rearrested. Judges apparently find the testing useful. Chief Judge Fred Ugast considers a test result "perhaps the single most important piece of information'' in determining conditions of release.

But civil libertarians have found several aspects of the program objectionable. First of all, the test used is the EMIT, and instead of confirming positive results with a more reliable test, a second EMIT is used. This can result in a double false positive and keep an arrestee in jail who would otherwise be out on bail. Civil libertarians also say that arrestees should be entitled to the presumption of innocence and to full Fourth Amendment protection. "We don't think that somebody who is innocent until proven guilty should be submitted to this kind of intrusive procedure," said Elizabeth Symonds of the ACLU's District of Columbia chapter. "I think it's also important to remember that this test doesn't tell whether someone is an addict."

Critics also complain that judges give the tests too much weight in bail hearings—because they appear scientific—and pay less attention to such other factors as ties to family and community or jobs. Finally, they say that District of Columbia drug treatment programs are filled to capacity and have three-month waiting lists, making officials' claims of rehabilitation meaningless. The ACLU has not yet found a suitable plaintiff to file suit against the program.

CHAPTER 5

Political and Social Issues

Many issues raised by drug testing are not addressed by courts, but by politicians, sports figures, leaders of industry, the press, and the public. To the extent that drug testing is legally permitted, such issues become especially important, because each of these groups will have a direct role in influencing whether testing will be implemented, and if so, how.

POLITICS AND TESTING

The national agenda for solving problems and making policy is largely set by our leaders, whom citizens look to for guidance. In September 1986, President Ronald Reagan significantly advanced the policy of drug testing. He signed an executive order calling for the testing of federal employees in "sensitive positions," including law-enforcement officers, Presidential appointees, and workers with access to classified information—as many as 1 million workers. "The use of illegal drugs, on or off duty, by Federal employees is inconsistent not only with the law-abiding behavior expected of all citizens, but also with the special trust placed in such employees as servants of the public," Reagan said in the order. He allocated $56 million for the tests. Around the same time, Congress enacted legislation increasing penalties for drug-related offenses and took other steps to "get tough on drugs."

In taking his action, President Reagan seemed to have the public squarely behind him. A *Newsweek* poll showed 75 percent of all Americans supported testing for government workers. In a *USA Today* poll taken in March 1986, 77 percent of respondents said they would not object to being tested in the workplace, and 62 percent supported mandatory drug testing for federal workers and employees of government contractors. Only 43 percent, however, favored private-sector testing, while 48 percent were against it. And an August 1986 *New York Times* poll found the public more hostile to marijuana than it was in 1977, with 57 percent saying that possession of small quantities of the drug should be treated as a criminal offense.

Responding to the *USA Today* poll, Carlton Turner, director of the White House Drug Abuse Policy Office, said, "What you're seeing overall is that the American public is saying, 'We're fed up—we're tired of drugs—and whatever it takes to do it, let's do it.' " One example of this was the attitude of Gretchen Brenner, a federal employee who worked in Kansas City, Missouri, as a Veterans Administration dental assistant. She said, "I don't care," that testing could violate her rights. "I didn't want to be forced to put a smoke detector in my home, but I felt it was for my own good."

Not everyone, however, felt that way. Many civil servants objected to the Reagan initiative. "I don't want my rights trampled because of mass hysteria over the drug problem," said LeRoy J. Robertson, a senior inspector with the Customs Service in New Orleans, who had worked sixteen years for the government. And Margaret L. Thompson, a lawyer with the Environmental Protection Agency in New York City, said, "When I was hired for this job, off-campus conduct was never mentioned as a condition of employment."

The *New York Times* poll revealed skepticism among the public regarding the intent of politicians on the drug issue. Sixty percent of them said most officials were making their antidrug proposals only for the publicity. Echoing this sentiment, Dr. William S. Greenfield, director of Addiction Treatment Services at the Presbyterian–University of Pennsylvania Medical Center, said, "Drug-testing of urine is a wonderful tool only for politicians." An editorial in the *Journal of the American Medical Association* labeled drug testing "Chemical McCarthyism" and pointed out that deaths and impairment caused by illegal drugs were actually already decreasing. Thus, it went on, politicians could "hype" the issue and then take credit for tackling a problem that was improving anyway.

Robert Ellis Smith, publisher of *Privacy Journal,* showed similar skepticism in his "Urinalysis of the 1986 Election." According to Smith, about sixty people running for major offices had asked their rivals to be drug tested, often after submitting to the procedure themselves. He said that such requests became a "farce," and the challenged politicians called them "a cheap political trick." One candidate for Congress in Pennsylvania, Marc Holtzman, waited three and a half hours for late CBS camera crews to show up so his provision of a urine sample would receive network coverage. The next day, the headlines in the local newspaper read, MARC URINATES FOR COUNTRY, NETWORK TV, and the politician was pictured holding up a jar of urine. He lost the election.

53

It is possible that President Reagan, Vice President George Bush, and many others on the White House senior staff had set the stage for this sort of stunt by submitting to urinalysis themselves and publicizing it. In an ironic twist, though, one person close to the White House refused to be tested. When Rodney Smith, deputy director of the President's Commission on Organized Crime, arrived at a congressional subcommittee hearing to discuss the commission's proposal for drug testing all federal employees, he was greeted by a surprising demand. Gary Ackerman, chair of the subcommittee, ordered him to go to the men's room and produce a urine sample, for testing, in front of an observer. Smith was indignant and said he should have been forewarned, while a fellow commission member protested that Congress had no right to make the demand unless it had cause to suspect Smith of drug use. Refusing to take the test, Smith nevertheless gave a statement to the subcommittee in support of unannounced urinalysis for drugs. Commenting on this incident as an illustration of "the underlying manipulation of power" in drug testing, columnist Charles Levendosky of the Wyoming *Casper Star-Tribune* wrote, "The message is clear, to paraphrase George Orwell in *Animal Farm,* 'All of us are equal, but some of us are more equal than others.' "

Some people angered by drug testing have organized imaginative protests. Students at Cornell University mailed sealed cups of urine to the President. Columnist Levendosky urged readers to send a piece of cardboard soaked in urine to the U.S. attorney general and to companies embracing testing. "Sound disgusting?" he wrote. "So is suffering the humiliation of having your privacy invaded."

Testing programs have also spawned businesses operated to subvert the screens. Jeffrey Nightbyrd of Austin, Texas, founded Byrd Laboratories, which he calls "the oldest purveyor of fine urine products in the United States." The lab sells "guaranteed drug-free" powdered urine and a pamphlet with instructions on how to beat drug tests. Nightbyrd maintains that he's motivated by civil libertarian concerns, and claims he gets many calls from people who take legitimate drugs like Advil and are worried about false positives. "I'm not promoting stoned workers in the workplace," he said, "I'm defending privacy. I'm not Timothy Leary, I'm Thomas Jefferson." Byrd's service was praised by Gara LaMarche, director of the Texas chapter of the ACLU, who predicted "a flourishing market in clean urine" as drug testing spreads.

In St. Louis, Missouri, two partners on the police force went into business offering confidential drug tests that people could take to see if their urine was "clean" in advance of an employment urinalysis. "We have witnessed the erosion of what we consider personal rights of the individual and we saw a need for a system of checks and balances," one of the partners said.

SPORTS AND TESTING

Like political leaders, sports figures are often looked to to provide a certain kind of leadership—especially as role models for youth. So the sports arena has become a focal point for the debate over drug testing. The sports industry has been beset by drug problems, and athletes have become leading targets for drug screening.

While athletes have, for the most part, accepted tests in cases where an individual is suspected, they have resisted management's attempts to usher in random drug testing. Sports officials contend that such testing is necessary. In announcing a drug-testing program for all major league personnel except the unionized players, baseball Commissioner Peter Ueberroth said he wanted the league to be a leader in eradicating drugs from society. He asked the baseball players union to go along with testing voluntarily, but it refused. Ueberroth made the announcement in the aftermath of the highly publicized trials of two accused drug dealers in Pittsburgh. There, seven baseball players giving testimony said that they and many other players had used cocaine in the course of the baseball season. Claiming that drug users were vulnerable to corruption—such as fixing games for gamblers—Ueberroth said, "The integrity of the game is everything."

As discussed in Chapter 4, the National Football League tried, but failed, to institute unscheduled drug testing for players. Commissioner Pete Rozelle argued that illegal drugs could become an economic problem if they tainted the league and alienated fans seeking wholesome entertainment. He also expressed concern for "the health and welfare of the players—those taking drugs and those injured by those taking drugs."

Drug testing of athletes has drawn much media attention, especially, of course, from sports writers. *New York Times* columnist Dave Anderson said of the baseball union, "By refusing to adopt mandatory testing, the players' association is protecting the guilty and increasing the ill, not protecting the innocent and harboring the healthy." He also argued that a player's right to privacy was inherently diminished: "He exists in public, in stadiums with thousands of spectators." And Dick Young, writing in the New York *Daily News,* said that New York Mets star first-baseman Keith Hernandez, one of the players to testify in Pittsburgh, should not win the 1986 Most Valuable Player award: "How do we let a kid think that it must be okay to do drugs because look at Keith Hernandez. He did it, and he's an MVP of the National League." *Sports Illustrated* took a poll on drug testing in sports and found that 73 percent of their respondents approved of it.

Other writers have stressed that athletes are only human, arguing that we have no right to hold them to higher standards than anyone else. *New York Times* columnist Tom Wicker wrote, "Do you want your son drooling tobacco juice, kicking dirt on umpires, throwing at batters' heads, spiking opponents? No one threatens mandatory programs to stop such role modeling." Opponents of drug testing in sports see it as demeaning and setting a bad precedent. *New Yorker* writer Roger Angell quoted an All-Star American League infielder who noted that yes, racehorses have their urine tested, but "I am not a horse." Angell wrote, "Compulsory testing in baseball, the national pastime, will become a symbolic, integral part of a national pattern of drug testing . . . part of a major alteration of our freedoms and priorities."

There is a middle ground in this debate. Some opponents of random urinalysis for drugs approve of the National Basketball Association's antidrug program, which tests players only upon reasonable suspicion. They say that this is the only fair approach, and it teaches the public appropriate lessons about civil liberties. Ira Berkow, applauding the testing procedure that led to the firing of two Houston Rockets players for cocaine use, wrote in the *Times,* "If the players are going to be role models for youngsters, then the league administration ought to be as well."

LEGAL DRUGS

Critics of drug testing in sports call it "grandstanding" on the part of management to get public support. They argue that it's hypocritical because it attacks drugs like cocaine and marijuana, while bypassing performance-enhancing drugs that could equally damage players' health. Novelist and former NFL defensive end Pat Toomay said after Pete Rozelle announced his random-testing plan, "All of a sudden he's worried. It's been going on forever. What about all those guys running around on amphetamines? Painkillers? Steroids? They didn't just start hurting people last season, you know."

Times columnist George Vecsey reminded readers that major league baseball made no plans to test for amphetamines, whose use, he said, was pervasive in the game. One player said the stimulants he took make "you feel much more alert and alleviate the pain somewhat. It makes your body feel stronger." While Ueberroth argued that amphetamines were legal, Vecsey implied that many players use them without a prescription, which is against the law.

The theme of opportunism and hypocrisy in drug testing comes up often, even outside of sports. For example, a major reason for the popularity of testing is the rise of cocaine use. But only a small proportion of people discovered by drug tests will be coke users. Instead, the overwhelming majority of them will be pot users, because so many people smoke marijuana and because its metabolites remain in the urine for so long. The National Institute on Drug Abuse (NIDA) estimates that about 90 percent of those discovered through urinalysis will be marijuana users, 5 percent coke users, and 5 percent users of other illegal drugs. Critics of testing say it is unfair for people to lose their jobs for a crime that would carry just a small fine in many states. Alaska has decriminalized pot altogether. Residents of that state can legally cultivate their own marijuana plants.

Most alcohol users are not affected by testing at all. Yet according to NIDA, since 1980 the number of alcoholics in America has increased by 8 percent, to 12 million. Alcohol abuse can greatly damage a person's health and impair performance. George Lundberg, editor of the *Journal of the American Medical Association,* called it hypocritical to focus testing efforts on illegal drugs while ignoring alcohol and tobacco. "People continue to die every day of both legal and illegal drugs, but much more of legal than illegal," he said. According to *Time* magazine, "more than any other ailment, alcoholism breeds absenteeism, high medical bills and reduced work quality." And Mark A. Rothstein, a University of Houston Law Center visiting professor and author of a book about employee medical screening, said that alcohol causes more problems in the workplace than all illegal drugs combined.

There is a wide generation gap in the perception of alcohol

and drug abuse. According to an August 1986 poll conducted by *The New York Times* and CBS, when asked, "Which is a more serious problem today?" 46 percent of people age forty-five and older said illegal drug use, and 21 percent said alcohol abuse. Nearly twice as many people eighteen to forty-four years old—39 percent—felt that alcohol abuse was more serious; another 39 percent of them said illegal drug use was more serious. Thus, it makes sense that the people implementing screening programs—who are likely to be older—would see testing for drugs as more important than attacking the alcohol problem. Drug-testing foes view this attitude with irony. Press critic Geoffrey Stokes noted that the publisher of the *Bergen Record* in New Jersey, who proposed drug testing for employees, was arrested for drunken driving—"proving that God has a sense of humor."

SOCIAL CONTROL AND MANAGEMENT/EMPLOYEE RELATIONS

To some critics, it makes sense that drug testing and other antidrug measures have largely ignored the alcohol problem. They contend that the real purpose of testing is not so much to fight drugs as to establish a kind of social control reminiscent of George Orwell's *1984*. *The Nation* editorialized that drug testing "isolates people [and] raises the general level of anxiety." Anxiety could be fostered by random testing—you never know when your boss will demand that you provide a sample. Isolation, critics say, is an effect of the intense antidrug atmosphere, of which drug testing is such an important part. This atmosphere can destroy basic trust between people, as in cases in which parents administer drug tests to their kids or young children turn their parents in to the police for possessing drugs. "This is evidence of drug-abuse hysteria," William Safire wrote, "as if the nation is high from its crackdown on crack." In an atmosphere like this, people become more submissive to authority, hence more easily "controlled" by their employer and their government. Workers are less likely to strike, citizens less inclined to protest.

But according to some people, exercising this kind of control isn't always in management's interest. They say that drug testing can poison the relationship between workers and management—destroying morale, which hurts both sides. One union official said that indiscriminate testing could result in employee protests: "How do you take little sainted Mary Murphy, who never had a problem, and in a random sample, ask her to come in and urinate in a urinalysis test, and not cause a revolution in your office or plant?"

Los Angeles management attorney Alfred Klein argued that employers could lose valuable employees. He noted cases in which a worker who used a drug casually left a firm in embarrassment after testing positive, even though the company wanted the employee to stay.

Some employers have avoided such situations by shunning drug tests altogether. The Ralston-Purina company, in St. Louis, has done this, saying, "When you require drug testing, it could be perceived that the company has a lack of trust in an employee. At Ralston-Purina, we place a lot of importance on that trust." And Joe Lanza, of Tulleytown, Pennsylvania, who owns a house-painting business, said he doesn't care what employees do in their own time, "as long as they work. A drug test is not fair. . . . If it affected their work, I'd think twice."

Opponents of drug testing say the fact that many flourishing businesses, large and small, have not turned to the procedure is evidence that it is unnecessary. To decrease the demand for illegal drugs, they suggest instead improving educational efforts to warn young people of potential dangers. Some also argue that we should be more concerned about the underlying causes of drug abuse, such as poverty and social breakdown. Others say that if resources were redirected from testing to law enforcement, we would stand a better chance of stopping drugs at our borders. Representative Patricia Schroeder of Colorado claimed that the United States could hire an additional twelve thousand law-enforcement agents at annual salaries of $25,000 with the money saved if federal drug-testing efforts were cancelled.

PART 2
Polygraphs

CHAPTER 6

How Polygraphs Work

*T*he human race has a long history of devising methods for determining when a person is lying and when he or she is telling the truth. Early societies used torture. Statements made by a person on the rack were considered especially believable. There was also trial by ordeal, which was based on superstition. For instance, if there were two suspects for one crime, it was thought that the innocent would be stronger in combat and thus vanquish a guilty opponent.

The ancient Hindus made suspects chew rice and spit it onto a leaf from a sacred tree. If they couldn't spit, they were ruled guilty. Although this procedure long predated the modern lie detector, it was based—knowingly or not—on assumptions about psychological stress much like those that support polygraph examinations today. The ancient test depended on the fact that fear makes the mouth dry, so rice would stick in a guilty person's mouth. For the procedure to work, the subject had to believe in its accuracy and, if guilty, had to be anxious about being caught in a lie.

The modern polygraph is said to measure the subject's "internal blushes" in much the same way. It does not really detect lies—only physiological responses. The theory behind the polygraph is that lying always heightens these responses. When taking the test, subjects are hooked up to a briefcase-sized machine by means of several attachments. Usually, a pneumatic tube goes around the chest to measure respiration, a cuff squeezes one bicep to monitor blood pressure, and electrodes are attached to two fingertips to determine the skin's resistance to electrical current (which is related to how much the subject is sweating). An examiner, or polygrapher, quizzes the subject. As the subject answers the questions, the machine draws squiggles on a chart representing physiological responses, which are supposed to clue the examiner in to the subject's lying, or truthful, ways. Just as the ancient Hindu was betrayed by a dry mouth, the modern polygraph subject is said to indicate that he or she is lying by breathing harder or having a racing pulse. (In arriving at a conclusion about a person's deceptiveness, some polygraphers also use their own subjective observations of the person's behavior.)

The test will not work, though, if the subject does not believe in the procedure. If the subject does not think the machine can tell the examiner anything, then he or she won't be anxious and won't show the heightened responses that the machine is designed to record. Because of this, the examiner will often use deceptive tricks to impress the subject with the polygraph's alleged accuracy.

Modern polygraphy got its start in Chicago in the 1930s, where it was used in criminal justice investigations. Now it has a wide range of other applications, including screening job applicants and employees, conducting intelligence investigations in federal security departments like the Central Intelligence Agency (CIA), and trying to uncover the source of unauthorized disclosures to the press of government documents or information.

The strategies used by polygraphers vary from one application of the machine to another. In pre-employment screens, subjects are typically asked a series of about twenty questions. "Irrelevant" questions like "Is your name Erica?" serve to put the subject at ease. Typical "relevant" questions are: Have you ever been convicted of a crime? Stolen from a previous employer? Is all the information on your employment application correct? Do you take illegal drugs? This series is repeated, and if physiological responses to particular relevant questions are consistently and significantly higher than responses to others, the subject is reported as "deceptive."

Investigations into specific incidents are more complicated. In these, "relevant" questions concern only the alleged wrongdoing—for instance, "Did you steal the missing $500?" To determine truthfulness, polygraph responses to these questions are compared with responses to other questions—called "control" questions—that are provocative but do not relate to the incident.

The use of polygraphs in the workplace greatly increased over the last fifteen years, and now over 2 million of them are given annually in the United States. Seventy-five percent of them are administered to job applicants. Other tests are given periodically or randomly to employees or as part of an investigation in the wake of a theft or act of sabotage. Although subjects technically submit to testing "voluntarily"—generally signing a release saying they are willing to undergo such an examination—they actually have few options. Applicants who refuse a screen are not likely to be hired, and even long-time employees who demur risk being fired or having their decision held against them in some way.

According to the American Polygraph Association (APA), an industry group that promotes lie-detector use, one-fifth of all major U.S. businesses use the machine in some capacity. The test is most commonly used by firms in which low-level employees handle large sums of cash, such as banks, restaurants, and department stores. But all kinds of concerns have tested their employees—from meat-packing companies to hospitals. Though some companies have in-house polygraph operations, most hire a security firm to do their lie detecting for them. Generally, companies using lie detectors make submission to testing a condition of employment.

Polygraphs are also sometimes used on state and federal government employees. The Department of Defense (DOD) uses the polygraph more than any other federal agency except the CIA and the National Security Agency (NSA). The DOD gave 25,000 tests in 1985. The department uses polygraphs for criminal and counterintelligence investigations and to screen people being considered for access to classified information. The CIA and NSA, which together have about 100,000 employees, screen all job applicants with the machine and also use it in investigations as well as in random checks on employees. No one refusing a pre-employment polygraph will be hired by the CIA or NSA. In 1979, three-quarters or more of the applicants turned down for CIA jobs were rejected because of their polygraph results. Sometimes the federal government also uses lie detectors to track down the source of unauthorized disclosures, or "leaks," to the press.

The U.S. Postal Service uses the polygraph more than any other agency not involved in national security. The primary use here is in investigations of mail theft.

The Office of Personnel Management strictly regulates pre-employment polygraph programs for many federal agencies. Its rules require that any agency doing screening have "a mission approaching the sensitivity of that of the Central Intelligence Agency." The questions asked in the course of the exam must be narrow, and the agency involved must monitor procedures "to prevent abuses or unwarranted invasions of privacy." The rules also require employers to tell the subjects that they have a privilege against self-incrimination and a right to consult a lawyer before the test, and, in addition, that refusal to submit to a lie detector will not be recorded in employment files.

The Defense Department has similar regulations governing polygraph use. Defense employees can refuse lie detectors used in investigations of criminal activities or unauthorized disclosures without suffering adverse consequences.

THE CASE FOR THE POLYGRAPH

In 1976, a southern California commercial bakery was in a bad fix. The retailers who bought its bread were finding pieces of glass and wire in the product, and they were furious. Company officials suspected sabotage. Desperate, they hired Intercept, a Hollywood company specializing in lie detection. Twenty-four hours after two polygraphers arrived, the bakery was back to normal. In the course of an examination, a longtime employee "owned up": Angered at being passed over for a promotion, he had done the vengeful deed.

In 1978, a gas station in Salt Lake City, Utah, called in Polygraph Screening Service to examine its workers. Two hundred and ninety dollars in cash had just been discovered missing, and the company had lost another $700 in cash and goods over the preceding month. During a "pretest interview"—the interview that examiners often give just prior to hookup with the polygraph—a worker confessed to charging customers for gas and then keeping the money instead of ringing it up on the cash register. After this worker was connected to the machine, his charts indicated strong responses to queries regarding the missing $290. He subsequently admitted that he had absentmindedly left the key in the cashbox during a trip to the lavatory. When he next checked the box, the money was gone.

These examples, taken from the book *A Tremor in the Blood: Uses and Abuses of the Lie Detector,* by professor of psychology David Lykken, illustrate the effectiveness and efficiency of the polygraph in solving some problems for employers. Employers are particularly concerned about theft, and some believe that the polygraph is the answer. The U.S. Chamber of Commerce says that "business executives view employee theft as their most serious crime problem." In a study by the U.S. Department of Justice of employees in electronics factories, hospitals, and retail stores, 30 percent said they stole from the company. Generally, losses due to theft are passed on in higher prices to customers. Some business groups say employee theft raises the price of consumer goods by as much as 15 percent. According to the Fireman's Fund Insurance Company, roughly one-third of all business failures are caused by employee theft. And estimates of the annual cost of economic crime against business, including employee theft, range from $67 billion to $200 billion.

The APA argues, "The best way to stop employee theft is simply not hire those employees inclined to steal. The best way is also impossible. What the employer must do is set up a screening process that will weed out the obvious security risks. Many experts believe that personnel screening is the most vital safeguard against internal theft." After passing polygraph screens as applicants, employees can then be polygraphed periodically—say, once every six months—or at random to deter them from criminal acts on the job. If a theft occurs nonetheless, the polygraph is a useful investigative tool. Not only can it be helpful in tracking down the culprit, it can clear an innocent employee who was incorrectly suspected.

The APA says that the majority of companies that adopt the lie detector cut internal theft by over 10 percent. Further, they get a better idea of whether or not an applicant is honest than they would from traditional means, such as checking references. The polygraph also lets them check the veracity of résumés and applications. (One Gallup poll on ethical behavior found that 49 percent of the general public has lied on employment applications.)

70

Polygraph proponents claim some great success stories: the case of Willoughby Peerless, a large East Coast camera store chain, for instance. Its Philadelphia store, suffering from inventory losses of about 14 percent, adopted the polygraph. The losses subsequently decreased to 1 percent. And a representative of the National Association of Convenience Stores testified at a congressional hearing that inventory theft from its 525 member companies could be reduced by half with the help of the lie detector.

The APA claims an accuracy rate for polygraphs of between 85 and 95 percent. Though the procedure is not infallible, its proponents say it is the most accurate way to get at the truth. Far more accurate, for instance, than relying on someone's unsupported subjective judgment. True, a victim of an inaccurate test may not be hired for a job, but companies basing their decisions solely on interviews and references make incorrect hiring decisions every day.

Besides, in a way the polygraph's validity isn't that important an issue. According to Lykken, about 90 percent of the adverse recommendations polygraphers give to employers are based on admissions of wrongdoing that subjects make in the course of an examination. Such confessions spare examiners the task of divining truths and lies from squiggles on a piece of paper. Polygrapher John Reid boasted, "We get better results than a priest does." The APA is opposed to firing an employee or charging a suspect with a crime solely on the basis of lie detector results. It says that most employers won't dismiss workers without some additional evidence.

THE CASE AGAINST THE POLYGRAPH

As with drug tests, critics of polygraph examinations say that even if they do serve to deter crime, their cost in individual rights outweighs any benefits. They believe lie-detector use to be unethical and sometimes illegal, and they are fighting it in the courts, in legislatures, and in union halls. These are some of their arguments:

▶ *Polygraph tests invade privacy.* Because examiners often ask personal questions not relating specifically to the investigation at hand. And even if the inquiries are appropriate, polygraph exams are "mental strip searches" that try to insinuate their way into a person's thoughts by continually monitoring his or her physiological responses.

▶ *Polygraphs are unfair.* Because the utility of the machines is in getting people to admit wrongdoing. But if they don't elicit a confession, the tests may be useless or produce "false positives," mislabeling truthful people as liars. A 1983 report on lie detectors by the Congressional Office of Technology Assessment (OTA) reviewed several studies of polygraph validity and found that the results of these studies varied widely—and reports of false positives reached as high as 75 percent. The OTA concluded, "There appears, as yet, to be no scientific field evidence that polygraph examinations can be effectively used to investigate unauthorized disclosures or that they represent a valid test to prescreen or periodically screen government employees." The OTA did find that the machines detected deception at a rate "better than chance" in specific-incident criminal investigations, but said that even here "significant error rates are possible."

Accuracy problems may be especially acute in private-sector screening, according to an aide to Senator Orrin Hatch of Utah, who has sponsored antipolygraph legislation. He said that often polygraphers will only spend fifteen minutes on these tests—as opposed to the four hours they may spend in testing for national security clearances—and that the examinations are biased against the innocent. "Nuns would fail polygraph tests, and convicts would pass them."

▶ *Many polygraph operators are incompetent.* A lawyer for an employee who had been fired because of a lie detector said, "In what is a very typical pattern, the polygrapher proved to be a retired police employee, and my cross examination of him proved that he knew very little about the supposed 'science' of polygraphy and could no more tell you who was telling the truth than a Ouija board."

▶ *Polygraphs do not enhance national security.* Because spies can be trained to beat the tests. And by going after government employees who have leaked information to the press, polygraphs foster censorship.

▶ *Polygraphs are an instrument of terror.* Because they are a modern version of interrogation under torture, with examiners using pressure tactics and intimidation to scare people into confessing. They create a climate of fear wherever they are used.

Like the drug-testing debate, the battle over polygraphs finds civil libertarians and labor unions in a face-off with public and private employers. With the passage of an antipolygraph bill by the House of Representatives in 1986, the critics seem to be winning. This was the closest that Congress had ever come to outlawing polygraphs in the private sector.

This legislation and other legal aspects of polygraph testing are discussed in Chapter 7. Chapter 8 deals with the political battle over polygraph testing in the federal government and with some broad social concerns raised by lie detectors.

CHAPTER 7

Legal Issues

*T*he Fifth Amendment to the Constitution states, "No person . . . shall be compelled in any criminal case to be a witness against himself." According to Nat Hentoff, a columnist for the New York *Village Voice* who specializes in constitutional liberties issues, this amendment has a longer history behind it than even our guarantees of free speech, the right to counsel, and the prohibition of unreasonable searches and seizures. Hentoff wrote that John Lilburne, a British Puritan who lived in the seventeenth century, was the "father of the Fifth Amendment."

In 1637, English authorities, outraged by Lilburne's printing and distribution of religiously dissident books, ordered him before the Star Chamber. In an attempt to extract a confession, they told him to sign an oath to tell the truth about his activities. Lilburne, a dedicated civil libertarian, refused to sign, saying, "I see you go about this Examination to ensnare me: for seeing the things for which I am imprisoned cannot be proved against me, you will get other [evidence] out of my examination." The young man was found in contempt of court and promptly put in a pillory, where he was gagged and whipped unmercifully, and then imprisoned. Lilburne's case received much publicity. In its aftermath, the English Parliament prohibited authorities from requiring anyone to "confess or accuse himself or herself of any crime."

In Old New York, under the Dutch, religious dissidents suffered ordeals similar to Lilburne's. But when the English took over, the right to remain silent became law. After colonial independence, this was deemed such an important right that it was written into the Constitution. According to constitutional scholar Leonard Levy, "The Fifth Amendment reflected [the Framers'] judgment that in a society based on respect for the individual, the government shouldered the burden of proving guilt and the accused need make no unwilling contribution to his conviction."

The Supreme Court has never specifically ruled on the self-incriminatory aspects of polygraph exams. However, in *Schmerber* v. *California* (see Chapters 2 and 3), it did touch on the issue. While holding that involuntary blood tests are not a form of self-incrimination, the Court indicated that other tests, such as polygraphs, that are "directed to eliciting responses which are essentially testimonial" may violate the Constitution in certain situations. "To compel a person to submit to testing in which an effort will be made to determine his guilt or innocence on the basis of physiological responses, whether willed or not, is to evoke the spirit and history of the Fifth Amendment."

Because the Fifth Amendment applies only in criminal settings, however, its application to employment is limited.

EMPLOYMENT

In a case not involving lie detectors that has since been applied to polygraph examinations by lower courts, the Supreme Court ruled that government employees—because of their responsibility to the public, who pays their salaries—could be required by employers "to answer questions specifically, directly, and narrowly relating to the performance of [their] official duties," provided there is no requirement to waive the constitutional privilege against compelled self-incrimination. Thus, a government employer may discipline an employee on the basis of statements made while under questioning, but the employer may not insist that an employee allow those statements to be used against him or her in court.

Many courts have permitted government employers to subject employees to polygraphs. But they have required that the employers comply with the Fifth Amendment when doing so. That is what happened in the Georgia case of *Hester* v. *City of Milledgeville,* which was decided by a U.S. district court in 1984 and then appealed to a higher court.

In this case, fire fighters employed by the city of Milledgeville sued to prevent their employer from subjecting them to polygraph tests. In March 1982, a Milledgeville Fire Department employee had been caught smoking marijuana in a fire station restroom, and there were other incidents revealing that fire fighters were using drugs. The chief of the fire department testified that in his opinion, by November 1983, 60 percent of the thirty-one fire department employees had used illegal drugs either on or off duty, and 20 to 25 percent had taken illegal drugs during work hours.

The city wanted to polygraph all fire department employees as part of their investigation of spreading illegal drug use. They planned to ask employees to sign a waiver giving up their rights against self-incrimination. Those who failed the test or refused to take it would be disciplined and possibly dismissed. But no one would be punished solely on the basis of his or her polygraph results.

The lead plaintiff was Freddie Hester, a fire fighter who had previously been polygraphed twice for unrelated reasons. He said that in each test the examiner had accused him of lying when he was actually telling the truth, so he did not trust the procedure. He and the other plaintiffs argued that since the polygraph was unreliable, it was unconstitutional for the city to fire them on the basis of test results. They alleged violations of Fifth and Fourteenth Amendment rights.

The defendants countered that a polygraph was a permissible way to investigate employee misconduct and denied that they were infringing on the workers' constitutional rights. They said that they were obeying the Supreme Court's requirements by asking ''narrow and specific'' questions.

U.S. District Court Judge Wilbur D. Owens, Jr., ruled in favor of the plaintiffs and issued an injunction forbidding polygraph use by the city. He said that under the Fifth Amendment, the plaintiffs could not be asked to sign a waiver surrendering their constitutional privilege against self-incrimination as a condition of continued employment. ''The important interests of . . . municipal governments in maintaining an honest . . . fire service do not justify infringing upon the more compelling interest that all persons have in the preservation of the privilege against compelled self-incrimination. . . .''

Owens noted that the city's polygrapher was using control questions unrelated to the narrow scope of the investigation—such questions as, ''While employed as a police officer, did you do anything that, if discovered, would have discredited your badge?'' or ''During the first twenty-one years of your life, had you ever lied to anyone who trusted you?'' These questions violated privacy and, thus, the procedure was impermissible. Owens also ruled that the polygraph was ''an invalid test'' whose use against the employees violated their due-process rights, as guaranteed by the Fifth and Fourteenth

Amendments. He supported his position that polygraphs are inaccurate by citing the 1983 report on lie detectors by the Congressional Office of Technology Assessment. The report said that there was no scientific proof that polygraphs are accurate in employment situations.

The defendants' claim that they would not use polygraph results alone as a basis for disciplinary action did not make the tests legal, he said. If there was other evidence, asked the judge, why bother with the exams in the first place? Further, the employer would surely keep polygraph reports of deceitfulness in mind when making future personnel decisions "in which plaintiffs have an interest protected by due process."

The defendants appealed this case to the Eleventh Circuit U.S. Court of Appeals, which saw the case somewhat differently. Writing for the court, Circuit Court Judge Vance agreed with Judge Owens that requiring employees to waive their constitutional rights was unconstitutional. Defendants could administer polygraphs, however, provided that employees kept their privilege against self-incrimination and as long as the fire fighters were not punished solely on the basis of the test results. Since the privilege against self-incrimination only applied to criminal cases, Vance said, it does not prevent a governmental unit from taking noncriminal disciplinary action against an employee on the basis of compelled testimony. He also found that control questions that went beyond the narrow scope of the investigation were acceptable because they were needed for accuracy—and this need outweighed the fire fighters' privacy rights. As for the employees' due-process rights, Vance found that these *were* protected by the employer's policy of not basing disciplinary action solely upon polygraph results.

But in some cases, public employees have successfully challenged the polygraph. Judges to whom they have brought their complaints have found the polygraph of questionable reliability or violative of privacy, regardless of procedures employers used to make the testing fairer. A U.S. district court in Texas, in striking down lie detectors for fire fighters because they violated privacy, quoted former Supreme Court Justice Louis Brandeis: "[The Framers of the Constitution] sought to protect Americans in their beliefs, their emotions, and their sensations. They conferred . . . the right to be let alone—the most comprehensive of rights and the right most valued by civilized men." And the Supreme Court of California ruled: "If there is a quintessential zone of human privacy it is the mind. Our ability to exclude others from our mental processes is intrinsic to the human personality." The court said polygraph investigations are never narrow. They always violate privacy, intruding continuously into the mind of employees by recording physiological functions against their will.

Certain inquiries are particularly invasive. Polygraphers for the Adolph Coors brewery asked job applicants: "What are your sexual preferences? How often do you change your underwear? Have you ever done anything with your wife that could be considered immoral? Are you a homosexual? Are you a Communist?"

University of Minnesota psychologist David Lykken, a polygraph critic, said, "Some of the stories have a truly Kafkaesque quality." Like the one about the military man of ten years' outstanding service and an unblemished record who had a strong reaction to a certain question. "What I'd suggest, Major," said the polygrapher, "is that you search your mind for anything you've thought or done in recent years that might be causing these reactions, anything at all that you're ashamed of. A kind of mental cleansing."

APA guidelines state that polygraphers should never ask irrelevant, intrusive questions. These include queries on a subject's religious and political beliefs, beliefs regarding racial matters, union activities, or sexual preferences. Polygraphers admit there are abuses, but say that proper licensing and regulation would end them.

Like the use of drug tests, polygraph use in private employment is not governed by the federal Constitution. However, private employers may not require an employee to relinquish his or her constitutional privilege against self-incrimination. Here again, civil libertarians urge private employers to follow the principles of the Constitution and abandon the polygraph on grounds of privacy and inaccuracy.

Because polygraphs have been in use in employment for a longer period of time than drug tests, state legislation concerning them is much more developed. This legislation generally applies to all private and most public employees.

About thirty states have passed laws requiring licensing or certification of polygraph examiners. This is the regulatory approach favored by the polygraph industry. Most laws require possession of a college degree, a period of internship, and successful completion of a licensing examination. Some limit the kinds of questions that an examiner can ask. In Illinois, for example, it is unlawful for examiners to make queries regarding a person's religious beliefs, sexual preferences, or political affiliations.

More than twenty states have laws curtailing lie-detector use in employment situations. There are several weaknesses in these laws, however. Many of them make exceptions for law-enforcement personnel and others in sensitive positions. And while all of them prohibit companies from ''requiring'' the tests, half of them permit firms to ''request'' that individuals take them. Critics say that employer pressure in ''request'' states can make workers feel that they have no choice but to take the test. They also say that companies in regulated states frequently test applicants in a nearby state where it is legal to do so. Violations of statutes are considered a misdemeanor and generally punished with only a small fine.

Civil libertarians and organized labor feel that only federal legislation would effectively curtail employment lie detectors. Several bills have been introduced in Congress, but so far none has become law. In March 1986, responding to critics' claims that at least fifty thousand people a year are wrongfully denied employment because of polygraph inaccuracies, the House of Representatives passed legislation barring lie detectors as a condition of employment in the private sector. It made exceptions for certain areas, saying, for instance, that power plant workers, private security guards, and employees of defense contractors who have access to classified materials could still be tested. So could public employees. The bill had support across the ideological spectrum—from Representative Jack Kemp, a conservative, to Senator Edward Kennedy, a liberal. But the White House threatened to veto the measure—on the grounds that federal regulation of polygraphs was a violation of states rights, and the Senate did not vote on it. The House defeated a substitute bill favored by polygraph advocates, which called for the licensing of polygraph examiners.

In addition to legislation, workers have a variety of other legal protections against and remedies for unfair treatment resulting from polygraph exams. For instance, critics cite mounting evidence that polygraphs illegally discriminate against blacks and other groups. An aide to Senator Orrin Hatch said that because of this evidence, courts will eventually bar the polygraph ''as a discriminatory pre-employment screening device.''

A recent court case in Chicago revealed that blacks may suffer the adverse consequences of polygraph errors more frequently than whites. In a discrimination suit brought in a U.S. district court, individuals seeking jobs as prison guards proved to the satisfaction of the court that blacks fail pre-employment polygraph tests more often than whites. Jon Bauer, a staff attorney for the Legal Action Center of New York, a public interest law firm that has litigated several polygraph cases, believes that the discrepancy may result from differences between blacks' and whites' physiological responses to stress, tensions between white examiners and black subjects, or prejudices that can enter into an examiner's evaluation, which may rely largely on subjective impressions. In any case, says Bauer, ''We should not tolerate a test that has a discriminatory effect on blacks when there is no adequate evidence that the test is valid.''

Some employers apparently use the polygraph to discriminate intentionally against blacks. Don Blews, a former manager for a department store chain in the Carolinas, testified about this in 1978 before a Senate Judiciary Subcommittee. According to Blews, his district supervisor told him that blacks "just don't work out" and ordered him to dismiss two black women workers. Blews said that when he refused, the supervisor remarked, "We'll have to show you how our polygraph works around here." The women were subsequently fired, their test results indicating "a sign of a possibility of deceit." His bosses also turned down the only two blacks whom he had ever recommended for management trainee positions, again on the basis of the polygraph test.

This kind of employment discrimination is illegal under federal and state civil rights laws, although it may be difficult to prove that an employer acted illegally.

Some state laws also protect the disabled against discrimination. These laws may protect the rights of people who stutter or have some other physical or mental condition that affects their physiological responses to the polygraph. And civil rights laws limiting what an employer may ask a job applicant apply equally to polygraph exams. Thus, in many states an examiner may not ask a subject questions regarding age, race, marital status, or arrests not leading to a conviction.

Some union organizers have found administrative hearings a means of fighting the polygraph. The National Labor Relations Board (NLRB) recently ruled on a case involving two waitresses who tried to organize a union at the Shoney's restaurant chain in Georgia. One of them, Maria Sganga, was fired on the basis of information she revealed during a pretest interview. The company said she admitted to taking home some leftover potatoes and parsley, a violation of company rules, even though she had her manager's permission. Patricia Burch, the other waitress, had refused to sign the test consent form, which in Georgia permits the examiner to inquire about a worker's finances and military service. She considered her finances her own business and didn't want to be questioned about the military because her husband was in the service. She offered to sign a revised consent form but was fired anyway, for actions her boss considered tantamount to refusing the polygraph test.

NLRB Judge Richard J. Linton ruled that Shoney's had "discharged Sganga and Burch because of their union and other protected . . . activities," adding that the company "would not have ordered the polygraph tests in the absence of such activities." He ordered the two women reinstated with back pay.

Unions generally have a low regard for polygraphs and say that in addition to harassing organizers with them, companies use the machines to screen out job applicants likely to join a union. Some unions protect their members, either by winning contract provisions forbidding polygraph examinations or by intervening to stop an employer from administering one. Further, union employees are usually protected by contract language specifying that they can be fired only for "just cause." Most labor arbitrators do not believe that refusal to submit to a polygraph exam or failing one constitutes just cause for dismissal.

Some nonunionized workers have been successful in bringing lawsuits against employers who used polygraphs. For instance, in 1982, an assistant manager in a department store in Florida received $250,000 as compensation for being fired under what the court called "circumstances implying that he had been guilty of a felony." He had failed a lie-detector test two years earlier and was dismissed for allegedly stealing $500 from the store. But after he left, the thefts continued, and eventually the culprit—who had passed the test—was discovered. The man sued the store for defamation and the company that administered the test for negligence.

Criminal Justice System

There are many stories of how the polygraph has helped law-enforcement officials get at the truth in carrying out investigations. In a California case, a fourteen-year-old girl accused her father of incest. When the man was polygraphed at the request of court officials, he was found to be truthful in his denial of the crime. His daughter then confessed: She had made up the story to punish her father because she was jealous of his multiple marriages.

A New Hampshire convict had a chance to persuade authorities of his innocence with a lie detector. After having served a few months of a 7-to-10-year sentence for allegedly raping his sister, he was polygraphed by a deputy sheriff. The deputy did not think the polygraph indicated deception when the man denied the crime, so he polygraphed the sister, and she failed. She subsequently confessed to fabricating the story in an attempt to protect her boyfriend: *He* was the one who had gotten her pregnant.

But for all the cases in which a polygraph helped investigators, there are others where it misled them. Take the case of Mark Hoffman, who submitted to a lie test in November 1985. He had been accused of setting two bombs, which killed two people, in an attempt to cover up an elaborate forged documents scheme. Police considered him their chief suspect, but Hoffman maintained his innocence. His attorney hired a lie-detector expert; Hoffman took a test and passed. For confirmation, the expert sent the polygraph charts to six people he considered the world's foremost lie-detector experts. Polygrapher David Raskin, who has tested such famous figures as Patty Hearst and John De Lorean, said of the charts, "The results were very consistent—everybody who looked at those charts agreed that they were truthful." Raskin announced publicly that Hoffman was innocent. But over a year later, Hoffman confessed. The police had been on the right track to start with!

How did Hoffman pass the test? One of the polygraphers involved said, "Our best guess . . . is that he is one of that small percentage of people who's able to pass the test even though they're lying." Raskin speculated that Hoffman may have intentionally employed techniques to fool the test. Studies have shown that people are sometimes successful in manipulating their physical responses—for example, by pressing on a tack in their shoe—to fool the test.

In an application that has been more controversial, polygraph results are sometimes admissible as evidence in court. This doesn't occur often, because most courts that allow polygraph results at all only permit "stipulated" results as evidence, which means both prosecution and defense must agree in advance to allow them. Courts are wary of lie-detector evidence because there is no consensus in the scientific community that the procedure is accurate.

The polygraph industry believes the machines should be allowed in court. David Raskin argues that, unfortunately, "the polygraph community has perpetrated a myth that these things are infallible . . . and therefore people expect perfection." But no evidence is foolproof, he says, and polygraph results don't have to be perfect to be useful.

Others disagree. The U.S. Department of Justice, while against outlawing polygraphs in private employment, opposes admissibility of lie-detector results in courtrooms. It says that a suspect can pick a polygraph examiner who will be biased in his or her favor, and also that juries, unduly awed by polygraphs, may disregard other important evidence.

And according to polygraph critic David Lykken, "If it has any legitimate role in the criminal justice system at all, the lie detector should be used exclusively—and circumspectly—in criminal investigation, aiding the search for the sorts of hard evidence traditionally admissible in court."

CHAPTER 8

Political and Social Issues

THE NATIONAL SECURITY QUESTION

The Reagan administration has persistently tried to expand the use of polygraphs to deal with press leaks and espionage. Despite strong resistance from Congress, the press, and the public, it has succeeded in more than doubling federal use of lie detectors. Reagan, however, was only speeding up a trend that had already been established. Between 1973 and 1983, the number of federal polygraph examinations tripled.

Reagan's efforts started in 1982, when the Pentagon sought congressional approval of a plan to expand its polygraph use. At the time, the Department of Defense was limited to examinations of employees carried out as part of criminal investigations. DOD officials wanted to expand examinations to include screening job applicants and random testing of employees; but Congress frowned on the idea. During that year, the Pentagon used the lie detector in a way it never had before: After embarrassing information was disclosed to *The Washington Post,* the agency rounded up and polygraphed thirty employees, including the chairmen of the Joint Chiefs of Staff.

In 1983, angered by more leaks to the press, Reagan proposed that all federal workers with access to classified information—a full half of the federal work force—should be possible subjects for polygraph investigations into unauthorized disclosures to the media. But protest from the press and public caused the President to back off.

Again, in 1985, Reagan sought to expand polygraph use—and the targets were now possibly to include Cabinet officers. When Secretary of State George Shultz got wind of this, he balked, saying that he would resign before taking a polygraph. The President then changed his mind.

But in the same year, in the aftermath of the John Walker spy case, the Pentagon did convince Congress to allow for some expansion of polygraph use. Walker, a retired communications specialist who worked for the Navy and was privy to sensitive national security information, was accused of forming a spy network that included members of his family. The network was said to have sold sensitive intelligence information to Soviet agents for several years before Walker's capture. The arrest got much attention in the press and spurred congressional approval of a pilot Defense Department polygraph plan, which called for the screening of some employees for sensitive security clearance.

Political debate over federal polygraph screening has involved questions of national security, the machine's accuracy, invasion of privacy, and censorship. Representative C. W. Bill Young of Florida, who introduced an amendment in Congress to expand counterintelligence lie detecting, said the tests were ''essential to preventing the transfer of important technology to the Soviet Union." He also said that doubts about the polygraph's validity and utility should be ignored because what mattered was that security officials found them "one of the best tools they could have to persuade someone with access to classified and highly sensitive national security information not to yield to the temptation to sell such information to a foreign power." He pointed out that though most people with access to sensitive information were honest, "one traitor . . . can cause serious and irreparable damage to our national security." Finally, he argued that regulations limiting the kinds of questions examiners could ask would prevent any violation of constitutional rights.

Several former espionage agents agreed that the polygraph is useful. Christopher Boyce, who was convicted of spying against the United States, said he wouldn't have done it had he been faced with a lie detector. While the tests might not stop professionals in espionage, he said, they "would have clearly affected amateurs like myself." While working for a defense contractor, he had applied for clearance to get access to top secret information. The government did a background check and found no damning information, so it cleared him. This was a mistake: "I know that if I had been polygraphed solely on attitudes toward the government and CIA . . . I probably never would have been considered for the job."

Soviet defector and former KGB agent Stanislav Levchenko said that the Soviet intelligence agency rarely sends its own sophisticated spies to penetrate other governments, but instead recruits foreign nationals to do its bidding. The Soviets cannot train these spies in sophisticated techniques like beating the polygraph, so "the more segments of the U.S. government that introduce polygraphing, the more difficult it will be for the KGB . . . to collect secret information on the political, economic, and military policies of this country." To illustrate this, Levchenko recalled a recent case in which the KGB chose to place one of their agents in the State Department rather than the CIA. The Soviets intentionally chose a department that did not use the polygraph for security clearances.

But opponents of expanding government polygraph use are concerned about the lack of evidence establishing lie detectors as accurate. They point, for instance, to congressional testimony given by Dr. John F. Beary III, associate dean of the Georgetown University School of Medicine: "The polygraph . . . detects excitement, not lying. Lying is only one of several stimuli which may excite a person. Other stimuli which cause excitement are fear of losing one's job, embarrassment, or anger at being examined."

Representative Jack Brooks of Texas said he had nothing against polygraphing suspects in criminal investigations, but called pre-employment and other screens of government employees "fishing expeditions [conducted] without any suspicion of wrongdoing." According to Brooks, Defense Department documents show that even if the polygraph is assumed to have an accuracy rate of 90 percent in screening, for every thousand persons tested, ninety-seven would be falsely accused of deception. Polygraph proponents, he said, apparently think that "if innocent people are mislabeled liars and traitors, that is acceptable in the name of national security."

Critics worry that spies who beat the test will be thought of as trustworthy and loyal. Columnist William Safire wrote, "skilled liars can fool the polygraph," and called the machine "a spy's best friend." Dr. Leonard Saxe of Boston University, who headed the Congressional Office of Technology Assessment's polygraph study, testified before a Senate committee: "Given that accuracy depends on the subject believing in the technique, maintaining a disbelief in the examination may be the most effective countermeasure." Saxe authored a second study that found that people who do not believe in the polygraph's effectiveness can lie without being detected.

Some say that the real danger is the false sense of security created in government agencies that rely on the polygraph instead of old-fashioned diligence. Representative Don Edwards of California criticized the CIA's lie-detector use, which failed to stop a clerk from disclosing the names of CIA informants in Ghana. The CIA had ordered the woman to stop dating a man who worked for the Ghanaian intelligence service. She continued nevertheless, and the agency failed to pursue it. A year later, the man forced her to give confidential intelligence information to him.

Ironically, while the polygraph did not prevent it, it was during a random lie-detector test that the clerk confessed to her breach of security. Thus, polygraph advocates use this case to argue for the utility of random screening.

Some are skeptical about promises that guidelines would protect privacy. A General Accounting Office survey turned up the lesson plan for the "Polygraph Examiner Training Course" taught at the U.S. Army Military Police School at Fort McClellan, Alabama. The plan, which had been used from February 1984 to November 1985 and then suspended, called for examiners to ask personal questions forbidden by federal law. Among other things, polygraphers were told to ask subjects: Have you ever had a mental breakdown? Have you ever associated with persons addicted to drugs? Do you have any foreign pen pals? Are you a name dropper? Have you ever belonged to any group which refused to swear allegiance to the United States? Have you ever received sexual stimulation in a crowded area?

Another concern is that polygraphs used to track down disclosures or "leaks" to the press have a chilling effect, decreasing the amount of information available to the public about the government. Senator Charles McC. Mathias commented on a national security directive intended to stop leaks, "The tension between the legitimate need to protect our government's secrets and the right of Americans to speak and write what they believe has repeatedly confronted us." While lie-detector proponents say the examinations are necessary to plug leaks of sensitive information, others argue that much information is classified unnecessarily and worry that polygraph tests will become overreaching. Said *Washington Post* reporter George Wilson: "In the real world of the Pentagon . . . virtually every piece of enlightening information bears some kind of classification cover. . . . Widening [polygraph] use would indeed make it more difficult for reporters, senators, representatives, government staff people, pressure groups and plain citizens to find out what is going on inside the Pentagon."

THE FEAR FACTOR

When polygraph proponents speak of the machine's "deterrent effect" in ending leaks to the press or preventing espionage or theft, they are referring to the fear created by its use. During the Watergate scandal, President Richard Nixon said, "I don't know anything about polygraphs and I don't know how accurate they are, but I know they'll scare the hell out of people." One employer echoed this thought, saying that he uses the polygraph "to keep people honest." The idea is that potential targets of testing will stay in line to avoid having to confront the device. Jay Harvey, director of legislation for the AFL-CIO's Food and Allied Services Trades Department, says that most employers take this approach; only a minority really believe that polygraph results are reliable.

The machine may be effective in eliciting confessions and deterring crime, acknowledged William Safire, but "so is the rubber hose and bright light that used to be known as the third degree. The polygraph, or fear implanter, is a modern instrument of mental torture: To force it on a suspect is to give him the fourth degree."

How does the polygraph create fear? According to Norma Rollins, formerly with the New York Civil Liberties Union (NYCLU), who has studied polygraph practices, stories of polygraphers who badger, bully, and trick subjects into confessing abound. One common practice is to tell subjects when the examination is over that their charts indicated deception, even though they did not. Many people, fearing the jig is up, will then admit to a wrongdoing. But they would have been cleared had they kept quiet. In situations where the subject is actually truthful and has nothing to hide, he or she must bear the humiliation of being falsely accused. Ironically, in situations like these, the examiner is the "deceptive" one.

Certain interrogation techniques are also intended to scare people into "talking." For instance, during an examination, a polygrapher put the following questions to a woman applying for a job as dressing room attendant in a department store:

Did you ever use drugs?

Did you ever smoke pot?

Did you ever steal?
[Reply: a 50-cent magazine when she was fifteen.]

Is that all? You must have.

Did you ever shoplift?

Never?

Are you married?

What is your husband's salary?

What is your rent?

Did you have a happy childhood?

Were you popular?

Did you lie about your employment record?

Why did you falter on the shoplifting question?

What are you holding back?

Why are you shaking?

One woman vomited after her polygraph examination, and another suffered an asthma attack. In complaints to the NYCLU, people have called the experience "demeaning," "shattering," and "demoralizing." One man who passed his test seemed to sum up these responses when he commented, "I felt like I was raped."

Some polygraph critics argue that there are many employers who, like Richard Nixon, see the instilling of fear, not as a liability, but as a hidden benefit of the polygraph. Polygraph critics say the underlying motivation of such employers is that terrorized workers are easier to control.

But some companies that have adopted the polygraph worry that this element of fear actually works against them. The NYCLU says that some polygraph users "express qualms that a policy of polygraph testing creates an atmosphere of permanent distrust and hardens employees' feelings of alienation from the company. These companies have said that it might be wiser to assure employee honesty by building employee loyalty." Many big companies, including J. C. Penney, Sears Roebuck and Company, IBM, and General Electric, do not use the polygraph. Some firms have abandoned the polygraph for narrow, practical reasons. The personnel manager of a fast-food chain called the polygraph "a hassle . . . an expensive practice that, for the most part, simply doesn't do what its advocates claim it can do."

CHAPTER 9

Conclusion

*T*here are many similarities between drug tests and polygraphs. Both are scientific or quasi-scientific tools for determining a person's guilt or innocence. Both became extremely controversial because of widespread use in employment. Now it is likely that more drug tests and polygraphs are used in employment than in all other applications combined.

The strongest argument against testing is that it may tread on our privacy. People antagonistic to the examinations point to abuses in test giving that occur in the real world. Those favoring them have a vision of an ideal world in which guidelines and regulations would stop abuses.

Civil libertarians bring the debate to its most theoretical level when they say that even without abuses, testing procedures are inherently intrusive. Employers and other authorities typically counter this assertion by claiming the intrusions are justified. A person will sympathize with one side or the other in this debate depending on his or her values. On the side favoring testing are the values of law and order and the rights of employers to run their operations as they see fit. On the side opposing testing are human dignity and workers' rights to just treatment.

Clashes of values in America usually end up in court, and testing has been no exception. In the public sector, judges must draw a line between the employee's Fourth Amendment, Fifth Amendment, and other privacy protections and the employer's interest in eliminating on-the-job crime. So far, nothing has been decided conclusively. The Supreme Court has not accepted any cases involving polygraphs or drug testing in employment.

The courts have been divided over providing workers with full Fourth Amendment protections. Thus, at this time, while some public employees may not be subjected to drug tests without good grounds for suspecting them of work-impairing drug abuse, others are not equally protected. Courts have generally given the go-ahead to polygraphs, provided that proper procedures are carried out. Several, though, have ruled that no matter what the procedures, polygraph tests are an unconstitutional invasion of privacy.

Drug tests and polygraphs also both raise questions about validity. The courts have found each procedure potentially inaccurate. Inaccuracies are more likely to be a legal problem in drug tests, because employers who use them often base their disciplinary actions on the results alone. In public employment, this raises due-process problems. The government may not deprive anyone of property without due process, and courts have ruled that public employees have a property right in their jobs. Several courts have struck down drug tests as violating due process. Most, however, have not found that polygraph tests violate due process, as long as the results are not the sole basis for disciplinary action.

Private-sector employers, in the absence of legislation, have considerably more leeway in testing programs. They can decide whether or not testing is in their interest. Some companies embrace one kind of test while rejecting the other. *The New York Times,* for instance, applauds drug testing and uses it in applicant screening. But it has editorialized against polygraphs because of their inaccuracies.

When deciding whether to test, private employers must ask themselves whether the benefits outweigh the costs, or vice versa. Employers adopting testing may face an increase in their insurance premiums because of the possibility of lawsuits stemming from testing improprieties. They may create bad will among employees made resentful by being subjected to tests. And they may lose valued workers as a result of inaccuracies. Other employers see an important deterrent value in the tests. They may be glad, too, to have difficult employment decisions reduced to the simple yes or no provided by testing.

So far, the majority of employers have not found testing in their interest and have not used it. Some employers will not test as a matter of conscience. Malcolm Forbes, publisher of *Forbes* magazine, has said that most drug and polygraph tests "are outrageous violations of privacy that should be illegal."

Ultimately, the extent of testing in employment may depend more on legislatures than on court decisions or employers' whims. Already, about half the states in the nation have some type of restriction on lie detectors, and most apply to public and private employees. Federal antipolygraph legislation, closer to passing than ever, would deal a critical blow to the lie detector. On the other hand, in the current antidrug political climate, it is unlikely that any federal efforts will be made to ban drug tests. However, a few states have passed such bans, and it is possible that drug testing legislation could develop the way polygraph legislation has.

If testing in employment were to be outlawed, what would the alternatives be? Some people, like polygraph critic David Lykken, say good management could do the trick. After all, businesses in America thrived before testing became popular, and many are doing fine without it today. In hiring, employers can check references and get other background information. On the job, they should be able to tell when workers are under the influence of drugs just by watching them carefully. To prevent theft, companies should keep good records, lock up valuables, and check inventory. Surveillance of employees is another possibility.

Ironically, many of these traditional techniques violate privacy too. *Privacy Journal* publisher Robert Ellis Smith said, "The alternative to polygraphs, you could say, is much more intrusive than polygraphs themselves."

One possible nonintrusive answer is the creation of policies that will increase employee goodwill. David Lykken suggests that employers adopt profit-sharing programs, "ideally [ones that are] focused on relatively small groups of employees who are in daily contact, so that each person will be encouraged to feel that to steal from the company is to steal from one's friends and colleagues." In a Senate survey of seventy-five firms, most that developed an employee stock-ownership plan greatly increased earnings and also avoided employee theft and sabotage.

There is more to employment testing than urinalysis and polygraphs. Although these are two of the most widely used tests, there are several other kinds, and many of them raise similar issues.

Some employers in states where polygraphs have been banned have turned to written "honesty tests." These use an applicant's yes or no answers to test questions to try to determine his or her predisposition to steal. A nun who applied for work in Minneapolis said she failed one of these tests with "the lowest score . . . they had ever seen." She testified in front of Minnesota's legislature, which decided to ban such tests.

Many employers administer pre-employment personality tests. These often ask extremely intrusive questions, dealing, for instance, with a person's toilet habits. Some industrial psychologists question the validity of the tests, but hiring decisions may be greatly influenced by them.

The U.S. Army, the State Department, and at least one private employer require testing for the AIDS antibody. People who test positive could be deprived of employment, even though the disease cannot be transmitted by casual contact in the workplace and not everybody with the antibody gets the disease.

Some chemical companies have performed genetic screening on workers to see if they have a susceptibility to certain environmental hazards. Employers have used the results of these tests to keep workers out of jobs in which they could be exposed to certain toxins. Yet the Office of Technology Assessment has said that the tests in use so far cannot predict what might happen on the job.

All of these tests have been cited by civil libertarians as violating privacy and being unfair. And as technology marches on, there will no doubt be many new kinds of tests that raise similar problems. So, long after we have resolved the question of how much drug testing and polygraphing we are willing to tolerate, there will likely be other clashes that involve testing and questions of constitutional and human rights.

SOURCES

*T*he following sources are listed roughly in the order in which the information they contain is first discussed in each chapter.

INTRODUCTION

"Quotable," *Privacy Journal,* March 1986, p. 2.

Francis J. Flaherty, "Truth Technology," *Progressive,* June 1982, pp. 30–35.

Alfonso A. Narvaez, "U.S. Judge Blocks Urine Drug Tests," *New York Times,* September 19, 1986, pp. A1, B2.

George Orwell, *1984,* New York: Harcourt, 1949.

Robert Ellis Smith, *Privacy: How to Protect What's Left of It,* Garden City, N.Y.: Doubleday, 1980.

Robert Ellis Smith, "Implanted Sensors to Measure Our Likes and Dislikes?" *Privacy Journal,* January 1987, pp. 3–4.

David Thoreson Lykken, *A Tremor in the Blood: Uses and Abuses of the Lie Detector,* New York: McGraw-Hill, 1981.

CHAPTER 1

National Institute on Drug Abuse, *Statistical Series: Annual Data, 1982,* U.S. Department of Health and Human Services, Washington, D.C., 1982.

Janice Castro, "Battling the Enemy Within," *Time,* March 17, 1986, pp. 52–61.

Bureau of National Affairs, *Alcohol and Drugs in the Workplace:*

Costs, Controls, and Controversy, Washington, D.C.: BNA, 1986.

New York Times, articles throughout 1985–86.

CHAPTER 2

Irving R. Kaufman, "The Battle over Drug Testing," *New York Times Magazine,* October 19, 1986, pp. 52, 54, 59, 64–69.

Schmerber v. *California,* 384 U.S. 757, U.S. Supreme Court, June 20, 1966.

Peter B. Bensinger, "To Fight Illegal Drugs, Millions Must Be Tested," *USA Today,* March 7, 1986, p. 10A.

Stephen R. Dujack, "Drugs at Work," *Common Cause Magazine,* November/December 1986, pp. 39–41.

Donahue transcript no. 03146.

Charles Levendosky, "Workplace Made Safe without Drug Tests," (Wyoming) *Casper Star-Tribune,* June 22, 1986, p. A10.

"ACLU Speaks Out! Drug Testing in the Workplace," American Civil Liberties Union flier, 1986.

Janice Castro, "Battling the Enemy Within," *Time,* March 17, 1986, pp. 52–61.

Bureau of National Affairs, *Alcohol and Drugs in the Workplace,* Washington, D.C.: BNA, 1986.

Sam Fulwood III, "Test of Workers a Thorny Case for Company Lawyers," *Baltimore Sun,* March 17, 1986, p. 5A.

McDonell v. *Hunter,* U.S. District Court, Iowa, 1985.

National Treasury Employees Union v. *U.S. Customs Service,* U.S. District Court, Louisiana, November 14, 1986.

Capua v. *City of Plainfield,* U.S. District Court, New Jersey, September 18, 1986.

Letter from U.S. Comptroller General Charles A. Bowsher to U.S. Representative William D. Ford, September 11, 1986.

"Army Veterans May Appeal Drug Test Punishments," *Veterans Rights Newsletter* (published by Veterans Education Project, Washington, D.C.), October-December 1984, pp. 41, 53–55.

New York Times, articles throughout 1985–86.

CHAPTER 3

Alexander Stille, "Drug Testing," *The National Law Journal,* April 7, 1986, pp. 1, 22–24.

Charles Levendosky, "Drug Tests Could Fire You, Innocent You," (Wyoming) *Casper Star-Tribune,* June 15, 1986, p. A12.

Bureau of National Affairs, *Alcohol and Drugs in the Workplace,* Washington, D.C.: BNA, 1986.

Capua v. *City of Plainfield,* U.S. District Court, New Jersey, September 18, 1986.

Stephen R. Dujack, "Drugs at Work," *Common Cause Magazine,* November/December 1986, pp. 39–41.

National Treasury Employees Union v. *U.S. Customs Service*, U.S. District Court, Louisiana, November 14, 1986.

New York Times, articles throughout 1985–86.

CHAPTER 4

Bureau of National Affairs, *Alcohol and Drugs in the Workplace,* Washington, D.C.: BNA, 1986.

Katherine Bishop, "Drug Testing Comes to Work," *California Lawyer,* April 1986, pp. 29–32.

H. G. Reza, "SDG&E Says Drug Test in Error, Worker Is Reinstated," *Los Angeles Times,* November 26, 1986, pp. 1–2.

San Francisco Board of Supervisors, Article 33A, December 1985. (Amending San Francisco Municipal Code.)

Richard R. Kasher, "Arbitration Opinion Involving Drug Testing in National Football League," Bureau of National Affairs, Washington, D.C., October 29, 1986.

Odenheim v. *Carlstadt–East Rutherford Regional School District,* New Jersey Superior Court, December 9, 1985.

Michael Rozansky, "Drug Tests for Students Ruled Unconstitutional," (Newark) *Star-Ledger,* December 11, 1985, pp. 1, 24.

"Becton Drug Tests: Parental Love vs. Liberty," (Bergen, N.J.) *Record,* June 24, 1985, pp. B1–B2.

"Arkadelphia School District's Use of Urine Test Ruled Unconstitutional," ACLU of Arkansas newsletter, October 1985, pp. 1, 11.

James B. Jacobs and Nadine Strossen, "Mass Investigations without Individualized Suspicion: A Constitutional and Policy Critique of Drunk Driving Roadblocks," *University of California, Davis, Law Review,* Spring 1985, pp. 595–679.

Robert Ellis Smith, "Sick 'Em Andy," *Privacy Journal,* November 1985, p. 2.

People v. *Richard T.,* California Court of Appeal, September 19, 1986.

Commonwealth v. *Trumble,* Massachusetts Supreme Judicial Court, October 15, 1985.

H. Laurence Ross and Graham Hughes, "Drunk Driving: What Not to Do," *Nation,* December 13, 1986, pp. 663–64.

Eric Neisser, "Legal Roadblocks to Traffic Roadblocks," *New Jersey Law Journal,* September 25, 1986, p. 6.

Kane v. *Fair*, Massachusetts Superior Court, August 5, 1983.

Interview with Elizabeth Symonds.

Phyllis Crockett, report on drug testing of juvenile arrestees in Washington, D.C., *Weekend Edition,* National Public Radio, December 13, 1986.

Peter Baker, "Superior Court Unveils Juvenile Drug-Testing Plan," *The Washington Times,* November 25, 1986, p. 6B.

Sam Meddis, "Program to Test Teen Offenders for Drugs," *USA Today,* November 25, 1986, p. 3A.

New York Times, articles throughout 1985–86.

CHAPTER 5

Stephen R. Dujack, "Drugs at Work," *Common Cause Magazine*, November/December 1986, pp. 39–41.

Sam Meddis, "The Message: 'We're Fed Up, Tired of Drugs,' " *USA Today*, March 7, 1986, pp. 1A–2A.

Dr. William S. Greenfield, "Drug Usage Has Many Forms—and Solutions," *Philadelphia Inquirer*, September 30, 1986.

Dr. George Lundberg, "Mandatory Unindicated Urine Drug Screening: Still Chemical McCarthyism," *Journal of the American Medical Association*, December 5, 1986, p. 3003–05.

Robert Ellis Smith, "A Urinalysis of the Election," *Privacy Journal*, November 1986, p. 5.

Charles Levendosky, "You *Can* Protest on-the-Job Drug Testing," (Wyoming) *Casper Star-Tribune*, June 8, 1986, p. A12.

Interview with Jeffrey Nightbyrd.

J. A. Lobbia, "Son of Reefer Madness," (St. Louis) *Riverfront Times*, January 7–13, 1987, pp. 1A, 6A, 8A.

Sandy Padwe, "Symptoms of a Deeper Malaise," *Nation*, September 27, 1986, pp. 276–79.

Roger Angell, "The Cheers for Keith," *New Yorker*, May 5, 1986, pp. 48–50, 55–65.

"What Is Our Drug Problem?" *Harper's*, December 1985, pp. 39–51.

Janice Castro, "Battling the Enemy Within," *Time*, March 17, 1986, pp. 52–61.

Katherine Bishop, "Drug Testing Comes to Work," *California Lawyer*, April 1986, pp. 29–32.

Geoffrey Stokes, "Press Clips," *Village Voice*, September 23, 1986, p. 8.

"The Crackdown," *Nation*, August 30, 1986, p. 131.

Bureau of National Affairs, *Alcohol and Drugs in the Workplace*, Washington, D.C.: BNA, 1986.

New York Times, articles throughout 1985–86.

CHAPTER 6

David Thoreson Lykken, *A Tremor in the Blood: Uses and Abuses of the Lie Detector,* New York: McGraw-Hill, 1981.

Norman Ansley and Stanley Abrams, *The Polygraph Profession,* Linthicum Heights, Md.: American Polygraph Association, 1980.

American Polygraph Association, "Polygraph: Issues and Answers," APA pamphlet (undated).

Francis J. Flaherty, "Truth Technology," *Progressive,* June 1982, pp. 30–35.

Edward Tivnan, "Truth and Consequences," *New York,* March 12, 1984, pp. 49–52.

Bureau of National Affairs, *Polygraphs and Employment: A BNA Special Report,* Washington, D.C.: BNA, 1985.

Robert Ellis Smith, "How the Polygraphers Impressed the Senators," *Privacy Journal,* January 1987, p. 2.

Robert Ellis Smith, "Just Published," *Privacy Journal,* January 1987, p. 8.

New York Times, articles throughout 1985–86.

CHAPTER 7

Nat Hentoff, "Colonel North's Right to Silence," *Village Voice,* January 13, 1987, p. 32.

Nat Hentoff, " 'For No Man Is Bound to Accuse Himself,' " *Village Voice,* January 20, 1987, p. 32.

Schmerber v. *California,* 384 U.S. 757, U.S. Supreme Court, June 20, 1966.

Hester v. *City of Milledgeville,* U.S. District Court, Georgia, December 11, 1984.

Hester v. *City of Milledgeville,* U.S. Court of Appeals, 11th Circuit, December 11, 1985.

Avila v. *City of Brownsville,* U.S. District Court, Texas, November 15, 1982.

Long Beach City Employees Association v. *City of Long Beach*, California Supreme Court, June 19, 1986.

AFL-CIO Food and Allied Service Trades Department (FAST), *Blood, Sweat and Fears: The Lie Detector Lie*, Washington, D.C.: FAST (undated).

Jean Cobb, "To Tell the Truth," *Common Cause Magazine*, September/October 1985, pp. 33–37.

American Polygraph Association, "Polygraph: Issues and Answers," APA pamphlet (undated).

Robert Ellis Smith, "How the Polygraphers Impressed the Senators," *Privacy Journal*, January 1987, p. 2.

Interview with Jon Bauer.

Hearings before the Subcommittee on the Constitution of the Judiciary Committee, U.S. Senate, November 15, 16, 1977, and September 19, 21, 1978.

Shoney's v. *Sganga and Burch*, National Labor Relations Board, May 11, 1983.

Ivey v. *Zayre Corp.*, Polk County, Fla., Circuit Court, June 13, 1980.

David Thoreson Lykken, *A Tremor in the Blood: Uses and Abuses of the Lie Detector*, New York: McGraw-Hill, 1981.

Howard Berkes, report on Mark Hoffman case, *All Things Considered*, National Public Radio, February 11, 1987.

Robert Ellis Smith, "Just Published," *Privacy Journal*, January 1987, p. 8.

New York Times, articles throughout 1985–86.

CHAPTER 8

Robert Ellis Smith, "Just Published," *Privacy Journal*, January 1987, p. 8.

Dorothy J. Samuels, "What If the Lie Detector Lies?" *Nation*, December 3, 1983, pp. 567–68.

Jean Cobb, "To Tell the Truth," *Common Cause Magazine*, September/October 1985, pp. 33–37.

Bureau of National Affairs, *Polygraphs and Employment,* Washington, D.C.: BNA, 1985.

"Quotable," *Privacy Journal,* January 1986, p. 2.

"Have You Ever Owed a Bar Bill?" *Harper's,* March 1986, pp. 14–16.

Interview with Jay Harvey.

Testimony of Norma Rollins before the Subcommittee on Employment Opportunities of the Committee on Education and Labor, U.S. House of Representatives, July 30, 1985.

New York Times, articles throughout 1985–86.

CHAPTER 9

Malcolm S. Forbes, "Fact and Comment," *Forbes,* February 10, 1986, p. 17.

Bureau of National Affairs, *Alcohol and Drugs in the Workplace,* Washington, D.C.: BNA, 1986.

David Thoreson Lykken, *A Tremor in the Blood: Uses and Abuses of the Lie Detector,* New York: McGraw-Hill, 1981.

Francis J. Flaherty, "Truth Technology," *Progressive,* June 1982, pp. 30–35.

INDEX

B

Baker, Russell, 35
Baseball, 55–57
Basketball, 57
Bates, Harold, 37
Bauer, Jon, 81
Beary, John F. III, 89
Beaulieu, Edith S., 42
Bensinger, Peter B., 22
Bergen Record, 59
Berkow, Ira, 57
Blacks, 81–82
Blews, Don, 82
Boyce, Christopher, 88
Brandeis, Louis, 79
Brenner, Gretchen, 52
Brill, Arthur, 23
Brooks, Jack, 89
Burch, Patricia, 82–83
Bush, George, 54
Byrd Laboratories, 54–55

C

California, 39–40, 41, 47
Cameras, security, 3–4
Campbell, Judith, 45
Carver, Jay, 49
Catlin, Don H., 32
Centers for Disease Control, 31

Central Intelligence Agency
  (CIA), 67, 68, 90
Chamber of Commerce
  (U.S.), 70
Ciolino, Peter, 44
Clark, Collette, 40
Cocaine, 9–10, 14, 31, 56,
  57, 58
Collins, Robert F., 27, 33
Commonwealth Edison,
  14
Computers, 4, 25
Congressional Office of
  Technology Assessment,
  72, 78, 89, 98
Constitution (U.S.), 18–22,
  25, 27, 39, 44
  See also specific amend-
  ments
Cornell University, 54
Crack. *See* Cocaine
Crime, 10, 84–85
Criminal justice system, 45–
  50, 84–85
Customs Service (U.S.), 27,
  33

D

Delaware v. *Prouse*, 47
Department of Defense
  (DOD), 68, 69, 86–87, 89

Symonds, Elizabeth, 50
Syva Corporation, 12, 31, 32

T

Teachers, 27
Television, 3
Theft, employee, 4, 5, 14
Thompson, Margaret L., 53
Time magazine, 58
Tobacco, 58
Toomay, Pat, 57
A Tremor in the Blood: Uses and Abuses of the Lie Detector, 69–70
Turner, Carlton, 52

U

Ueberroth, Peter, 55–56, 58
Ugast, Fred, 49
Unions, 41, 42–43, 83
Urine tests, 1
    accuracy of, 31–33, 37, 40, 42, 50
    constitutionality, 26
    and due process, 31
    of government employees, 18, 53, 54

of job applicants, 41–42
of jockeys, 28
as measure of impairment, 24–25
in military, 15, 31
under observation, 15–16, 22–23, 45
and politics, 53–54
in prisons, 25–26, 48–50
and privacy, 2, 15–16, 23, 54–55
procedure, 12
in schools, 44–45
in sports, 57
of teachers, 27
in workplace, 11, 14, 35, 39–43, 60

V

Vance, Judge, 78
Vecsey, George, 57–58
Vermont, 42
Vietor, Harold, 25–26

W

Walker, John, 87
Walsh, Michael, 15, 33

ABOUT THE AUTHOR

Daniel Jussim, a graduate of Vassar College, is a freelance writer living in New York City. His articles have appeared in *The Nation, Maclean's,* and *New Age.*